Sheila Bolton.
Reading.
October 28th 1980.

THE PRONUNCIATION OF ENGLISH
IN CANNOCK, STAFFORDSHIRE

PUBLICATIONS OF THE PHILOLOGICAL SOCIETY
XXIX

THE PRONUNCIATION OF ENGLISH IN CANNOCK, STAFFORDSHIRE

A Socio-Linguistic Survey
of an Urban Speech-Community

CHRISTOPHER D. HEATH,
Ph.D. (Leeds)

*now Head of the French Department
at New College, Telford, Salop*

Published for the Society by
BASIL BLACKWELL · OXFORD
1980

ISBN 0 631 11611 7

This book is published with the assistance of the
British Academy, which the Society gratefully
acknowledges.

Set in Great Britain by the Gloucester
Typesetting Co. Ltd. Printed and bound by
Billing & Sons Ltd., London, Guildford
and Worcester

Preface

In carrying out the survey which is described in the following pages, it was necessary to handle the social information and the linguistic information independently of each other. This has meant that the first few chapters may seem to have little connection with each other, so a summary of the book is presented here.

The first chapter explains the background to the survey and describes how a random sample of the population of the area was taken. The text of the linguistic questionnaire is also included.

Chapter II begins the detailed work by classifying the informants according to their social, educational and geographical background.

Chapter III is an excursus on the subject of modern phonological theory, the purpose being to show why an unusual system of transcription is used in the present work.

Chapter IV returns to the main theme and shows how, from the speech of those informants who had lived their whole life in the district, a basic 'local accent' could be defined. This local accent is then described in detail, and contrasted with the Received Pronunciation of English.

In the fifth chapter, certain features of pronunciation which differ in the two systems are used to classify the informants by purely linguistic criteria. This process is independent of the background classification in Chapter II. On the basis of these results, the informants are grouped into five linguistic classes.

Chapter VI brings together the results of Chapters II and V: in it the results are subjected to statistical tests, designed to show what correlations there may be between speech behaviour and the background of the informants.

Chapter VII discusses the results of the statistical tests and draws some conclusions from them about the factors which seem to influence the variations in speech behaviour among the informants.

The last chapter, which is not directly based on the survey, compares the results with known features of the dialects of rural Staffordshire. There is also a brief section on morphology.

In order to present the main argument more clearly, the bulk of the tabular material is collected in the appendices.

I should like to express my gratitude, first to the eighty anonymous informants who permitted me to intrude on their time for what must have seemed to them to be a crazy exercise; to Mr. C. J. Hill for his help and guidance concerning the statistical treatment of the data; and especially to Mr. Stanley Ellis of the University of Leeds, who guided every step of this research and gave valuable advice and encouragement.

June, 1979.

Contents

LIST OF TABLES

LIST OF VOWEL CHARTS

MAPS (at end of book)

Map 1: local government boundaries in South Staffordshire at the time of the survey (1967).

Map 2: local government boundaries in South Staffordshire as altered with effect from 1st April 1974.

Map 3: the Urban District of Cannock with place-names. The grid used in selecting the informants is superimposed on this map (see also page 9ff.).

Note on Phonetic Transcription

Only in a few cases have detailed articulatory descriptions of speech-sounds been given in the following pages: for the most part such descriptions may be readily deduced from the narrow phonetic transcription employed. The symbols used are those recommended in *Principles of the International Phonetic Association* (IPA), and the reader is assumed to be familiar with them.

In narrow transcriptions of RP, the account given by A. C. Gimson in *An Introduction to the Pronunciation of English* is followed, but with a few changes in symbolization:

(a) The IPA symbols ι and ο are used in place of ɪ and ʊ respectively.

(b) [ɐ], rather than [ʌ] is used to transcribe the usual RP pronunciation of the vowel of *cup*, *nut*, etc. This is to break with tradition, but it is done in the interests of accuracy, and also to avoid confusion, since in many non-RP accents a vowel similar to [ʌ] occurs.

(c) [ə:] is used instead of [ɜ:] to transcribe the vowel of *bird*, *curd*, etc.

The phonetic symbols are supplemented by diacritic signs where necessary. In the following examples the diacritics are applied to the vowel [e] and the consonants [k] and [n].

ẹ   a slightly closer tongue-position;
ɛ̣   a slightly more open tongue-position;
ë   a slightly more central tongue-position;
e̫   accompanied by lip-rounding;
e̱   a slightly retracted tongue-position;
e̟   a slightly advanced tongue-position;
ĕ   shorter duration than normal;

ṇ   functions as syllable-peak;

ṇ̊   wholly or partially devoiced;

k'   accompanied by aspiration;

ḵ̟   an advanced (fronted) tongue-position;

ḵ   a retracted tongue-position.

Where necessary diacritics may be combined, and this may mean altering the usual position in some cases.

CHAPTER I

General Introduction

This book is a revised form of a doctoral thesis submitted to the University of Leeds in February 1971. The object of the underlying research was, at its inception, somewhat vague: to find out more about the speech of the present writer's home town, Cannock in Staffordshire. For the benefit of those readers who are unfamiliar with the town, we must begin this account of the work by describing the area that was studied. The maps at the back of the book should be consulted.

The Cannock Chase District lies in South Staffordshire; Cannock town centre is about nine miles north-east of Wolverhampton, eight miles north-west of Walsall, ten miles south-east of Stafford and ten miles west of Lichfield. It is just outside that part of the West Midlands industrial zone which has long been called the 'Black Country'.

It has been necessary to give distances from the centre of Cannock, because the area studied here is a large one, of very irregular shape. Defining this area is additionally complicated because the survey took place between two series of boundary changes.

The field-work (that is the interviewing of informants, a process which will be described later in this chapter) was carried out between the autumn of 1967 and the early summer of 1968—except for one particularly elusive informant, a farmer who refused to take part until after harvest, so that his interview had to be delayed until November. As will be explained later, the survey was based on the current electoral roll, for which the qualification date was 10th October 1966. Now it is obvious that to use the electoral roll one must be working in a precisely defined area, and this survey took place within the boundaries of what was then the Urban District of Cannock.

Urban districts were created by the Local Government Act of 1894. A glance at Map 3 shows that this one includes not only Cannock itself but also other centres: Chadsmoor, Hednesford, Heath Hayes, Bridgtown. These and other places were once separate little towns or villages, but they have gradually been linked by industrial and residential development during this century. Cannock proper lies in the south-west corner of the district.

The first alteration in the Urban District boundary was a side-effect of the reorganisation of the Black Country boroughs on 1st April 1966. As a part of this, the nearby urban districts of Brownhills and Aldridge were amalgamated, except for one ward of Brownhills which was transferred to Cannock. On the qualification date, this ward had been part of Cannock Urban District for six months, and is therefore included in the survey; it comprises the village of Norton Canes, which supplied several informants, and a large area south of Watling Street (A5), partly rural, partly derelict, and so sparsely populated that it is not represented at all in the survey.

Since the survey was completed, boundaries have been changed yet again, this time as a result of the reorganisation of local government in 1974. The old distinction between urban and rural districts has now been abandoned, and counties are divided into units in which an attempt is made to balance town against country. In the area under review, the Black Country towns have been detached from Staffordshire and, together with Birmingham and Coventry, form the new West Midlands Metropolitan County. Cannock has not been absorbed into the new county, but is now incorporated into the Cannock Chase District of Staffordshire, which also includes the old Urban District of Rugeley and the parish of Brindley Heath. These latter areas are *not* included in the present survey.

To summarise, the area of the survey is the old Urban District of Cannock, within the boundaries of 1966 to 1974. We can divide this area, very roughly, into a western half which is now almost entirely built up, and an eastern half which was still quite rural when the survey was made. Since then, there has been a considerable increase in residential and industrial development in this part of the district, and current projects, notably a 'mini-town' to be sited between Cannock and Heath Hayes, are rapidly transforming the area. If the survey were repeated today, the eastern half of the district would yield many more informants than it did in 1967.

To the west of Cannock is open countryside; Shoal Hill, an off-shoot of the Chase, is a local beauty spot. Cannock Chase itself, an area of Forestry Commission plantations and open heathland, lies to the north and is part of the new district. Map 1 shows four parishes, Great Wyrley, Cheslyn Hay, Huntington and Burntwood, which until 1974 were parts of rural districts, although recent development has made them almost completely urban. In spite of their affinities with the Cannock Urban District, they have never been part of it, and so do not come within the scope of the survey.

Although people are much more mobile nowadays, the bulk of the population of Cannock still seems to be of local origin. (The evidence for this statement will be presented later.) But within the last twenty years there has been a considerable influx of people from other parts of the country. There is continual overspill from the Birmingham area; and in the early 1960s, many miners and their families came into the district from Scotland and Tyneside, as coalmines were being closed down there. The current development proposals, already referred to, are increasing this movement, and now, twelve years after the survey began, the population is not nearly as homogeneous as it then was.

For many years the mining industry has been the main source of employment in Cannock; and in spite of rapid closures of pits and the setting up of new forms of light industry, it is still basically a mining area.

This, then, is the region that is the subject of this book. Before going on to explain exactly how the survey was carried out, it is necessary to account for the fact that research into the speech of towns is comparatively new.

The words *accent* and *dialect* are used, often rather loosely, when describing the differences in speech between the various regions of a country. In this book the term *accent* will be used to refer only to features of pronunciation, whereas a *dialect* will be considered to be a regional form of a language, English in this case, with its own sound-pattern (*phonology*), grammar and vocabulary. The accidents of history have elevated one dialect into a position of prestige: this is *Standard English* which was originally the dialect of London but is now spoken by many millions throughout the world. The prestige *accent* (of England only), technically called the *Received Pronunciation* (RP), is taught to foreign students although, even in England, the majority of those whose grammar is that of Standard English do not use the Received Pronunciation.

The fact that there are regional varieties of English has been noted for centuries, and we have written comments on the situation dating from the Middle Ages. At that time, a standard language had not yet developed, and the available evidence indicates that dialectal differences were greater than they are today, so that Englishmen from different parts of the country often could not understand one another. Caxton, in 1490, illustrates this point with the famous story of the northerner who asked for *eggys*, and was not understood by the southern housewife whose word for these things was *eyren*.

The development of a standard language was a phenomenon of the fifteenth and sixteenth centuries. It is hardly surprising that it should be the speech of the capital that gained prestige; this is a natural process, and is paralleled by similar developments on the continent. The rise of London English was encouraged by the invention of printing, which made it possible to spread the standard language throughout the country. This dissemination was further assisted by the issue of officially sponsored publications in connection with the Reformation: the Book of Common Prayer (1549, 1552, etc.) and the English Bible (Great Bible 1539, Bishops' Bible 1568, Authorised Version 1611).

From the sixteenth and seventeenth centuries we have a number of books which illustrate differences between London and provincial English, sometimes scorning the countryman, sometimes treating regional accents in a more sympathetic manner. This literature is surveyed on pages 35–46 of *English Dialects—An Introduction* by Martyn Wakelin, who also quotes the text of Caxton's story about the eggs.

Can we say anything about the speech of towns in this period, as distinct from that of the country? The sharp contrast between urban and rural areas, with which we are familiar, did not then exist, and there is little reason to suppose that the speech of Bristol, Norwich or other provincial cities would be markedly different from their surrounding regions. There is no need to elaborate on the chief cause of the change in this situation: beginning gradually with the Industrial Revolution of the eighteenth century, and becoming ever more pronounced in the nineteenth and twentieth, a gulf has opened between town- and country-dwellers. One even hears stories of town children who had never realised that peas had an existence prior to being frozen in packets; such tales may be apocryphal, but are symptomatic of the lack of understanding.

It is not, of course, the mere existence of the town that is responsible for this situation, for civilisation means living in towns; it is the growth of mile upon mile of sprawling conurbations that has made it very easy for a town-bred child to be reared in complete ignorance of how the rural 'other half' lives.

When the study of regional speech became established on a scientific basis in the late nineteenth century, the already well-established urban areas were largely ignored, and the new science of *dialectology* became exclusively concerned with the country districts. Naturally one asks why.

This was the period when linguistic study meant above all research into the history and evolution of languages and dialects. By 1900, most of the details of development of the major European languages, including English, had been established. For scholars whose interest lay in reconstructing earlier stages of languages, dialects and regional accents had the same kind of function that fossils had for palaeontologists: they were surviving testimony to the accuracy of their theoretical speculations. This may be the explanation for the neglect of the speech of towns: the big industrial cities were comparatively recent creations, whereas the rural dialects could point back to the English of medieval or even Anglo-Saxon times.

The effect of this evolutionary attitude was an overwhelming historical bias in dialectology. This bias was reflected in its methods, which have changed little from the pioneer work of A. J. Ellis and Joseph Wright at the beginning of this century to the recent *Survey of English Dialects* conducted by Leeds University. The investigator seeks out a small village, well away from the commuter belts of cities, and in that village he selects the oldest inhabitants he can find who may be of use to him. For preference, the people he interviews for source material (his *informants*) will have spent their whole lives in the village. The reason for this approach is clear: only in this way can the investigator hope to obtain speciments of pure dialect, unadulterated by outside influences. Above all, the researcher wants to avoid people whose speech might have been affected by Standard English or the Received Pronunciation.

This last point is a reminder that one of the spurs to dialect study is the fear that the pervasive influence of the standard language may bring about the disappearance of regional varieties of English. The growth of mass-communication in our own century has accentuated the desire to record as much dialectal speech as possible while there is still time, an attitude which clearly reinforces the already existing historical bias.

In modern times, dialect study has frequently taken the form of comprehensive surveys of whole countries, the results usually being presented in atlas form. This type of systematic research began in Germany, but the first major work was Gilliéron's *Atlas Linguistique de la France*, published between 1902 and 1912. This example inspired similar studies in other countries, on both sides of the Atlantic, but no such survey was planned in England until after the Second World War.

The Survey of English Dialects (S.E.D.) was the result of collaboration between Professors Harold Orton of Leeds and Eugen Dieth of Zurich. Between them they constructed a linguistic questionnaire which, after being revised in the light of experience, was used by the field-workers on the survey, carried out between 1948 and 1961. The final form of the questionnaire was published in 1952.

A number of rural communities were selected in each English county, so that the whole country was covered—with the notable exception of the industrial conurbations and their immediately surrounding regions. Eleven centres were picked in Staffordshire; the nearest to the Cannock district were the villages of Mavesyn Ridware, Lapley and Himley (St 7, 8 and 11 in the coding used in S.E.D.). Mavesyn Ridware and Lapley are shown on Map 1. The field-work on Staffordshire was carried out by Peter H. Gibson, and as well as being incorporated in the survey was written up into an M.A. thesis under the title *Studies in the Linguistic Geography of Staffordshire*. Those parts of his work which are relevant to our subject are discussed in Chapter VIII.

The results of the S.E.D. have been published in several volumes of basic material, and have recently appeared in atlas form.

As well as scientific research into dialect, there has been a continuing popular interest, often fostered by the local press. The Cannock area is no exception. Over a period of years the *Cannock Advertiser* carried occasional articles by Mr. Eric Roberts, a county councillor, under the title *O'd Hedgfud* (a traditional local rendering of Old Hednesford). In these stories various elderly characters meet in the pub or barber's shop and reminisce about what life was like in their young days. The conversation is full of local words and expressions, and is spelt in such a way as to suggest the local accent. Councillor Roberts has published two books of collected stories under the titles *Bilberry Pie* and *More Bilberry Pie*. (Bilberries grow wild on Cannock Chase and families go out to pick them on summer evenings.)

So the Cannock area has its traditional local speech, and it is tempting to do a conventional dialect study on it: by finding a few elderly informants, tape-recording their conversation, and using the Dieth-Orton questionnaire to elicit features of pronunciation, grammar, phraseology, interesting items of vocabulary and so forth. But we are dealing here with a town, not an isolated farming community, and if the *O'd Hedgfud* characters were ever typical of the district, they certainly are no longer. Towns are socially complex structures, and the techniques that have been so successful in the study of rural dialects would produce distorted, and therefore invalid results if applied wholesale to a town. More practically, since a large proportion of the items in the S.E.D. questionnaire assume a lifetime's involvement in agriculture, most urban informants would be unable to respond at all. Two examples:

(What do you call) a row of mown grass? *Swath*.
What is it (i.e. what is the sheep called) until the second shearing?
Gimmer. (Questionnaire, pages 56 & 59).

At one time items of vocabulary like these were in the normal experience of the common people, but for reasons already given townsmen now grow up in total ignorance of this aspect of life.

Even the study of rural speech has not been exclusively concerned with the search for a sample of 'pure' dialect. Forty years ago, Helge Kökeritz, in *The Phonology of the Suffolk Dialect*, studied an area strongly influenced by the speech of London, and expressed his intentions in this way:

My intention has been to paint a true and faithful picture of the Suffolk dialect as now spoken, not to give an idealized and beautifully retouched photograph of the speech habits of very old people to the exclusion of those of the younger generation.

Again, G. L. Brook, in 'The Future of English Dialect Studies', quotes Kökeritz with approval and comments:

> . . . it is well to remember that the older rural dialects are not the only forms of speech that are worthy of study. (. . .) The process of change from the older to the newer forms of dialect is itself a worthwhile subject of study. How far is it possible to detect differences between the speech of older and younger members of the same community? (*Studies in honour of Harold Orton*, p. 17.)

If, as Kökeritz says, a study of 'pure' rural dialect is idealised, such a study of an urban area would be utterly misleading. Cannock is a case in point: although characters of the *Bilberry Pie* sort do still exist (the present writer met one extremely garrulous raconteur), the proportion of them in the present-day population must be exceedingly small. Not one appears in the random sample which forms the basis of this research.

A further and very obvious objection to the purist approach is that, since all the informants have to be old people, the results would be half a century out of date. Yet again, to restrict study to one age-group makes it impossible to attempt to answer Professor Brook's question.

There have been a few studies of urban dialect along the traditional lines of rural dialectology (W. Viereck: *Phonematische Analyse des Dialekts von Gateshead-upon-Tyne*; Eva Sivertsen: *Cockney Phonology*) but new approaches have also been devised. Examples of this are the work of William Labov in New York, Barbara Strang and others on Tyneside, and Charles Houck in Leeds. Recent work on urban speech is described in Wakelin, op. cit., pages 59–62.

The precise objective of the research into Cannock speech emerged from the considerations already discussed. It has been: to carry out a statistical survey of patterns of pronunciation in Cannock Urban District at the present time; to describe variations in speech over the whole community, and not just a selected part of it; and to relate the linguistic results, as far as possible, to the social, economic and geographical background of the various strata of the population.

The reader will notice that the field of study is restricted to the pronunciation of English in Cannock: we are concerned here only with *phonology*. There are two reasons for this: first, that to attempt to describe grammar and vocabulary as well would have made the task overwhelming; and second, because there is no reason to suppose that Cannock speech is much different in these respects from

South Staffordshire speech in general. As already mentioned (page 6), Gibson's thesis contains a full description of the speech of rural Staffordshire; in this book we are concerned only to describe the Cannock *accent*. Since Gibson's work is not generally available (except to the extent that his results appear in the *West Midland Counties* volume of S.E.D.), the results of the Cannock survey are compared with his in a later chapter.

The reason for investigating the background of the informants is that, before beginning work, it is likely that social factors will be involved. If the sample is to be representative, the informants must include all types, from doctors to labourers, from clergymen to housewives. Nobody expects his dustman and his bank manager to speak in the same way, even if they are both locally born. And they may well not be: the higher social classes are known to be more mobile, so our sample will include people who were not born in the area, some perhaps who have not been there very long. But because they form an element of the population, they have every right to be included in the survey, if an accurate picture of the linguistic situation in the town is to be obtained.

Having disposed of preliminary matters, we can now turn to an account of the Cannock survey itself.

The method used in establishing a random sample of informants was based on Charles Houck's procedure in Leeds. In order to be statistically valid, the sample had to be representative both of the population and of the component 'villages' of the Urban District. A densely populated area should yield more informants than a thinly populated one.

The starting-point was a map of the whole Urban District, marked with the National Grid. Using the Grid as a basis, the District was divided into squares, each of $\frac{1}{4}$ sq. kilometre in area. There were 220 squares, and each one was numbered, starting in the north-west corner and counting in the natural manner from west to east and from north to south.

Next, some idea of the population of each square was needed. For this use was made of the 1:2500 scale Ordnance Survey maps, on which each house is marked. Many squares, especially in the eastern half of the district, turned out to be uninhabited, or to contain only a few houses. Clearly it would be pointless to take one informant from each square: such a procedure would give Little Wyrley (a few farmhouses) as high a representation as Hednesford, a town of several thousand inhabitants. It was decided to set a minimum number of houses which would entitle a square to be included: the decision could only be arbitrary, but fifteen was chosen as the limit (counting a pair of semi-detached houses as two). This drastically reduced the number of squares to 94.

The 'rejected' squares could not be excluded from the survey, so each was joined up with the next lowest numbered selected square; e.g. if square 54 had more than fifteen houses, and squares 55 and 56 both had less, then these three squares would be amalgamated. This produced a pattern of squares and rectangles, which was renumbered in exactly the same way as before. There were 94 areas and the intention was to select one informant from each.

The informants were promised anonymity; to safeguard this, each informant is referred to only by the number of the area in which he or she lived at the time.

The next requirement was a list of all the inhabitants of the Urban District. The nearest thing to this is the register of electors, which was used as the basis of the sample. It has the advantage of not including people who may be just 'passing through' the area, but it also restricted the sample to adults. As already mentioned, the sample was taken in the autumn of 1967, using the current electoral roll, for which the qualification date was 10th October 1966. At that time the voting age was still twenty-one. The total electorate in that year was 34,423, so the ninety-four potential informants constituted a 0·27% sample.

The actual informants were selected by means of a random number table (a list of five-digit numbers thrown out entirely at random by a computer). It appeared that none of the 94 areas contained more than 600 houses; since most houses are occupied by two electors, 1,200 was set as an upper limit for the random numbers. Taking the areas in order, a random number less than 1,200 was assigned to each. Next, it was necessary to list all the streets and parts of streets in each area in alphabetical order, then count through the names in the appropriate part of the electoral roll, until the random number for that area was reached. This process provided the names and addresses of prospective informants.

In some of the more thinly populated areas, the list of electors was exhausted before reaching the random number; in such a case the count was restarted from the beginning.

The next stage was to approach the informants in turn, not knowing whether they would agree to help in what must seem to the layman to be a curious exercise. To assure them of my *bona fides*, a few days before calling on a potential informant, the following letter was sent from Stanley Ellis of the University of Leeds:

> English Language Section,
> School of English,
> The University of Leeds,
> Leeds 2.

Dear Sir/Madam,
            I am writing to ask for your help in a piece of University Research work being done by a Cannock schoolmaster, Mr. Christopher Heath.

Your name has come out from a total of about a hundred as a result of a careful selection made on a completely automatic method rather like that used by ERNIE, the Premium Bond number selector. The electoral roll of Cannock Urban District was used as the basis for the choice and Mr. Heath now needs an opportunity to spend a little time with you, it need not be more than half an hour, to ask you some very ordinary and simple questions which will show him certain features of your speech. It will also be a great help if you will give him some very brief details about your earlier background, if you were born in Cannock, or where you were at the age you learned to speak, and so on.

Names will not figure in the finished research work, all people who help will be given a number which will identify the information given, your name is important as a means of getting in touch with you in the first place.

Mr. Heath will call on you in the next few days in the hope that you will be able to help him, either when he calls, or by making arrangements for a later visit.

I do hope you will feel able to help Mr. Heath in his studies, which should be of great importance for the study of the varieties of English language we are now making.

> Yours sincerely,
> STANLEY ELLIS, M.A.
> Lecturer in English Language.

P.S. I am asking Mr. Heath to add his own signature to this letter so that you may have some means of identifying him if you should desire it. He carries a personal letter of identification signed by me and himself.

Signature of Mr. Heath . . . .

It is perhaps curious that only one informant asked to see the letter of identification.

Of the ninety-four prospective informants, eighty were successfully interviewed. Of the fourteen who were not interviewed, numbers 32, 81 and 90 had died since the electoral roll was compiled, nos. 27 and 58 had left the district, nos. 6, 17, 24, 47, 59, 70, 79 and 94 refused to assist for various reasons; and no. 2 was visited half-a-dozen times before the attempt was abandoned. In any case, this represents an 85% success rate, which is more than adequate for the needs of the survey.

In all statistics quoted from now on, this figure (80 informants) will be taken as the total. Details of sex and marital status are shown in the following table:

TABLE 1

	Single	Married	Widowed	Total
Men	0	42	2	44
Women	1	32	3	36
Total	1	74	5	80

The reason for there being only one single person is probably an effect of using the electoral roll. One had to be twenty years of age to be included (as a 'Y' voter) and two years had elapsed by the time the last interview was made. The youngest informant was twenty-three at the time of interview.

The next problem was to decide what linguistic material should be elicited from each informant.

In his survey of Leeds, Charles Houck used a questionnaire designed to elicit local equivalents of the sound-units (*phonemes*) of the Received Pronunciation, which will from now on be referred to by its usual abbreviation of RP. Gerry Knowles, in an unpublished paper, criticised Houck's approach on the grounds that it would show up areas where the Leeds system is poorer than that of RP, but fail to detect situations where it is richer. For many years it has been a commonplace of linguistics that the field-worker must proceed without any preconceptions about what he is going to find, in order to avoid the risk of overlooking something significant but unexpected.

This rigorous approach is most closely associated with the structural linguistics of the United States in the 1940s and early 1950s, and it is hardly surprising that it should have been developed there at that time. The leading figures in linguistics had mostly been trained to study and analyse American Indian languages which had not previously been reduced to writing. These languages exhibit an astonishing diversity, and any approach with preconceived ideas had to be ruled out. But there is little value in pretending that a researcher who studies an English dialect should artificially put himself in that situation, as if he were a field-worker going into the jungle, armed only with a tape-recorder and a copy of Kenneth L. Pike's *Phonemics*. Granted that he ought not to make up his mind beforehand about what he expects to find, there can be little danger in having ready-formulated ideas about what he might NOT expect to find. It would be pointless to proceed on the assumption that some 'exotic' sound might be encountered; the probable variations among English dialects are too well known to make such an approach necessary. For example, nobody is likely to compile a phonological questionnaire for an English dialect that would cater for the possibility of finding a bilabial click with phonemic status—clicks are not known in English (as speech-sounds), so the likelihood of finding one in a local accent is so remote as to be safely negligible.

The remarks in the last paragraph apply to any Englishman studying any English dialect; the present writer, as a native of Cannock, thinks it unlikely that anything significant has been overlooked.

As for Knowles' criticism of the use of RP as a basis, there really is no practicable alternative. RP is the only English accent that is fully described in books easily available to the general public; there is no option but to use it as a point of reference. But that is the only reason for using RP in this way; it is not superior to other varieties of English—such value-judgments have no place in linguistic research.

For the Cannock survey it was decided to elicit equivalents of all the RP phonemes, but to do so in all contexts which could conceivably modify the phoneme in question, regardless of whether it is actually modified in that context in RP or not. In this way it was hoped that no distinctive contrasts of any informant's speech would be missed.

Consider as an example the RP phoneme /g/ as in *good*, a voiced lenis velar stop. Before a front vowel it may be palatalised to some degree; in final position it may be devoiced. So in the survey it was necessary to include words which would test these possibilities. In some languages, e.g. Spanish and some dialects of German, inter-vocalic /g/ may undergo lenition; this does not normally happen in RP, but it might conceivably happen in some Cannock speech, so a word to test for it had to be included in the questionnaire.

In order to acquire supplementary material, each informant was asked to count up to ten before starting the questioning, on the pre-text of checking the recording level, and the machine was left on throughout the process. After the interview, everything that the informant had said was transcribed, not simply the words in the questionnaire. Some were of course more talkative than others, but the additional material acts as a useful check.

The questionnaire comprised seventy-one questions. In each case a sentence was read to the informant, except for the last word, which he or she had to supply. This meant that each key-word was uttered with the same sentence-final intonation. The order was deliberately scrambled so that the informant would not realise in advance what sounds were wanted.

Some of the items are similar to those used by Houck in Leeds, but there has been no insistence on 'minimal pairs', which form a minority of the vocabulary and cannot be regarded as a basic feature of a phonological system. Full use has, however, been made of the traditional /b-t/ and /b-d/ frames for eliciting vowels, since there are numerous short words of this form; they are useful for testing the effect of final consonants on the preceding vowel.

This introductory chapter concludes with the full text of the questionnaire. In each case, the final italicised word is the one to be elicited.

The Questionnaire

1. If, in the course of a conversation with somebody, he said something you didn't understand, you might ask: 'What are you talking *about*?'
2. When a policeman has a special area to patrol, you'd say he was walking his *beat*.
3. On a day when the weather isn't warm, and yet not really cold, you might say it was *cool*.

4. When they are children, most little girls have a plastic model of a child, which they can dress up with tiny clothes. This is called a *doll*.

5. Every person has two parents, a mother and a *father*.

6. Before a flower has a blossom, it will have a *bud*.

7. The opposite of boy is *girl*.

8. The front part of the bottom of a shoe is called the sole, and the back part is called the *heel*.

9. Men who are out of work would go along to the Labour Exchange to try and find a *job*.

10. If you were hunting a dangerous wounded animal, and your guide warned you to keep out of the way, you might say: 'No, I want to be in at the *kill*.'

11. The opposite of cow is *bull*.

12. (Indicating) This part of the body is called a *leg*.

13. There's a street in London with Buckingham Palace at one end of it. It's called The *Mall*.

14. There's a very famous river in Egypt called the *Nile*.

15. There are two things you would have put in a car at a garage. One is petrol, the other is *oil*.

16. You sometimes hear people say about a dog that its bark is worse than its *bite*.

17. If something broke on anything mechanical, you'd go to the shop for a spare *part*.

18. Nowadays, plastic flowers are made so well that they look almost *real*.

19. If somebody doesn't know the correct way to write simple English words, you'd say that he can't *spell*.

20. There's a saying that goes: You can't see the wood for the *trees*.

21. Suppose I've got two pieces of wood. One is one foot square; the other is two feet square. So the second of these is the *bigger*.

22. The opposite of a virtue is a *vice*.

23. The opposite of narrow is *wide*.

24. (Showing a yellow card) The colour of this card is *yellow*.

25. A place where different kinds of foreign animals are kept (there's one at Dudley) is called a *zoo*.

26. A fisherman goes out in a *boat*.

27. Today a dog bites; yesterday he *bit*.

28. In schools, the teachers usually write on a blackboard with *chalk*.

29. If the sky is completely covered with cloud the weather can be described as *dull*.
30. (Indicating) This part of the body is called a *finger*.
31. (Showing card with two pin-men on it) This man is in front, so this one is *behind*.
32. Most people keep their car in a *garage*.
33. When a child goes to a secondary school, the work he has to do gets *harder*.
34. If somebody tells you a joke, and you think it's funny, you'll probably *laugh*.
35. In order to get the right amount of each ingredient when cooking, you'd use a *measure*.
36. When ladies go out for the evening, they often wear round their neck a string of *beads*. And one is called a *bead*.
37. In the house, you'd grow flowers like geraniums in a flower *pot*.
38. If you were writing with a pencil, and you made a mistake, you'd erase it with a *rubber*.
39. Round their shoulders, old ladies often wear a *shawl*.
40. In the country, you sometimes see old cottages with roofs made of straw. This is called a *thatch*.
41. You might say that identical twins are as like as two peas in a *pod*.
42. At the bookmakers, you can place a *bet*.
43. Waltz, quickstep and foxtrot are all different kinds of *dance*.
44. Wines, spirits or water, are usually drunk out of a *glass*.
45. If you're looking for something, and you can't find it, you might say to yourself: ' I wonder where it's been *put*.'
46. An auctioneer holds up a valuable painting and says ' Ladies and gentlemen, what am I *bid*?'
47. If you had roast beef for Sunday dinner, you might eat it with Yorkshire *Pudding*.
48. If you were playing cricket, you'd try to hit the ball with a *bat*.
49. In most houses, the dirty water goes down the *drain*.
50. After tea or supper, you'd tell the small children it's time for *bed*.
51. If you were to go to America, you'd travel across the Atlantic in a *ship*.
52. The opposite of rich is *poor*.
53. If you took a newly-purchased object home, you might say: ' Look what I've just *bought*.'

54. If a few people are having tea, and you want to ask one of them to handle the tea-pot, you might say: 'Who's going to *pour*?'
55. The opposite of good is *bad*.
56. The opposite of body is *soul*.
57. I'm wearing shoes; if they came up to my ankles you'd call them *boots*. And one is called a *boot*.
58. If you went to a shop to pay a bill, the shopkeeper would write on the bill the word *paid*.
59. A man playing the piano in a pub would probably get the people there to *sing*.
60. The windows of a jail are usually *barred*.
61. Two things that usually go together: bread and *butter*.
62. A person who sings is called a *singer*.
63. And when he's actually doing it, you'd say he is *singing*.
64. (Showing card with 'Herbert' on it) A short name for the name on this card is *Bert*.
65. If you were cooking, you'd roll the pastry out on a *board*.
66. After the referee had made an unpopular decision against the home football team, the crowd *booed*.
67. A little flying creature with feathers is called a *bird*.
68. If you saw someone with legs bent like this (demonstrating) you'd say his legs were *bowed*.
69. When a man deliberately doesn't shave, you'd say he was growing a *beard*.
70. If you'd done something wrong, and somebody was ticking you off about it, but you weren't really bothered, you might say: 'I don't *care*.'
71. At a funeral or memorial service, you'd stand with your head *bowed*.

Cognates of the RP vowels and diphthongs followed by fortis plosives were elicited by: *eight*, *beat*, *bite/vice*, *about*, *boat*, *boot*, *thatch/bat*, *bet*, *bit/ship/six*, *pot*, *put*, *part*, *Bert*, *bought/chalk*.

Cognates of the RP vowels and diphthongs followed by lenis consonants were elicited by: *paid/drain*, *bead/trees*, *wide/five/nine*, *bowed* (68 and 71), *booed*, *bad*, *bed/leg/ten*, *bid*, *pod/job*, *bud/rubber*, *pudding*, *father/harder*, *bird*, *board*, *beard*.

Cognates of the RP vowels and diphthongs followed by 'dark L' were elicited by: *heel*, *Nile*, *soul*, *cool*, *oil*, *Mall*, *spell/yellow*, *hill*, *doll*, *dull*, *bull*, *girl*, *shawl*, *real*.

Cognates of the RP unstressed weak vowel /ə/ were elicited by: about, bigger, rubber, finger, etc.

Cognates of RP unstressed final /əʊ/ were elicited by: yellow.

Cognates of the RP centring diphthongs were elicited by: care, poor, pour; the last two being included to see if there is any contrast.

The occurence of cognates of RP /ɑ:/ or /æ/ in certain words was tested by laugh, dance, glass.

Cognates of RP initial /p/ and /b/ and of final /t/ and /d/ were elicited many times over in the questionnaire. Special items were included to obtain examples of the other consonants.

In initial position: spell, ten/two, chalk, trees, kill, cool, doll, dull, job, drain, garage, girl, five/father/finger, thatch, soul/six/seven, shawl, hill/harder, vice, zoo, Mall, Nile/nine, leg, real, wide, yellow.

In intervocalic position: rubber/about, harder, bigger, behind, measure, finger/singer/singing, garage.

In final position: ship, thatch, chalk, job, garage, leg, sing.

The phonemic status of the velar nasal was tested by: finger, sing, singer, singing, pudding.

CHAPTER II

The background of the informants

The previous chapter explained the aims of the survey of Cannock speech, and how it was carried out. When the last informant had been interviewed, in November 1968, there were two sets of material: linguistic information elicited by means of the questionnaire printed on pages 14 to 17, and background information on each informant, which was obtained in the course of the preliminary conversation. The next stage was to classify these two sets of material, in isolation from each other; then later, by comparing social facts with linguistic facts, it was hoped to discover some correlations between them.

This chapter classifies the background information on each informant. The raw information is presented in Appendix I, in a very condensed form; the following pages show the patterns that emerged from the data.

Sex

The figures for sex and marital status have already been given (page 12). There is no evidence that getting married affects one's speech in any way, but it will appear later on that sex is a factor to be considered. Of the eighty informants interviewed, 55% were men and 45% women; the details are to be found in column A of Table 26a (page 99).

Age

This question was quite simply (or tactlessly) put: 'Do you mind if I ask your age?' Nobody objected, so column C of Table 26a gives exact ages. But, for reasons which will appear in Chapter VI, the chi-square statistical test gives unreliable results if classes with a very small membership are used. So for classification purposes, the informants were grouped into three age-ranges:

(1) *Young*: ages 21 to 40. There were 31 informants in this range, comprising $38\frac{3}{4}\%$ of the total.

(2) *Middle-aged*: ages 41 to 60. 30 informants, $37\frac{1}{2}\%$ of the total.

(3) *Elderly*: ages 61 and over. 19 informants, $23\frac{3}{4}\%$ of the total.

The youngest informant was 23 and the oldest 79.

Schooling

Each informant was asked what kind of school he or she attended, and at what age he or she left school. The leaving ages range from twelve to eighteen. Naturally, the significance of any particular age of leaving school depends on what the statutory minimum was at the time. The Education Act of 1918 fixed the school-leaving age at 14, and the 1944 Act raised it to 15, although this provision did not come into force until 1949. (The provision in the 1944 Act for eventually raising the leaving age to 16 had not been implemented at the time of the survey; the change took place in 1972.) What is significant, then, is how long an informant stayed on at school beyond the minimum leaving age of the time. On this basis, they are classified as follows:

(1) *Left at the minimum age:* 67 informants, $83\frac{3}{4}\%$ of the total.

(2) *Stayed for up to three extra years:* 13 informants, $16\frac{1}{4}\%$ of the total.

No distinction is made here between different extents of extra schooling, because the small numbers involved make such fine details unsuitable for statistical testing. For those who are interested, the informants concerned are nos. 18, 28, 29, 35, 37, 46, 50, 51, 60, 61, 65, 86 and 91. The details are given below:

TABLE 2

Extra years	Informants could have left school at			Total
	13	*14*	*15*	
1	3	1	1	5
2	1	1	1	3
3	1	3	1	5
Total	5	5	3	13

Clearly, the vast majority of the informants had left school as soon as possible. The most common type of school attended was the elementary school in the case of older informants, and the secondary modern school in the case of younger ones.

Income-group

Income is a delicate topic to ask people about. The informant was asked to do no more than say into which grouping his annual income fell; the groups being of £500 as given in column E of Appendix I. No informant objected to answering this question; several freely gave their weekly wage. A few informants were unable to answer this question. Since only five informants had annual incomes in excess of £2,000, only two large classes were used, with £1,000 as the dividing line. Most of the pensioners come in the lower group, as one would expect. The figures are:

(1) *Less than £1,000 per annum:* 37 informants, $46\frac{1}{4}\%$ of the total.
(2) *More than £1,000 per annum:* 39 informants, $48\frac{3}{4}\%$ of the total.
(3) *Income not known:* 4 informants, 5% of the total.

There is no need for comment on the changes in the value of money!

The geographical information

Columns G to M of Appendix I give a wealth of geographical information about each informant. In the event, little use was made of the birthplace of the informant's mother and father, except in one matter which will be explained in Chapter IV. The most useful information was the informant's own birthplace, and the list of residences.

In the first chapter, it is mentioned that the population of Cannock is no longer as static as it used to be (page 3). In view of this remark, it may seem surprising that $38\frac{3}{4}\%$ of the informants had spent their whole lives within the Urban District (excluding military service in the case of some of the men). The reason is probably that in 1967 the change in the character of the district was only just beginning. Classifying the remainder of the informants was rather a problem: a large number were born in such places as Huntington, Great Wyrley, or the other parishes shown on Map 1—technically these places are outside Cannock Urban District, but in terms of

building development they are continuous with it, and their inhabitants are linguistically associated with those who have
spent their lives in Cannock. Other informants were born elsewhere in the West Midlands, and have therefore a slighter affinity
with Cannock speech; and some were born in distant parts of
the country—these include two Scots, two Northumbrians and a
Welshwoman, each with the distinctive accent of their place of
origin.

At this point we have to anticipate some of the results of the
linguistic side of this enquiry. It will be shown in Chapter IV that
the varieties of pronunciation to be found in Cannock can be grouped
into several classes, ranging from approximations to the Received
Pronunciation at one extreme to what may be called a 'Cannock
accent' at the other. There are no boundaries between these classes
—they form a continuum, and any dividing lines have to be to some
extent arbitrary. However, there are four informants, the two
Scots and two 'Geordies' mentioned above, whose speech has no
place in this continuum. They have a strong accent of their own,
and have been in Cannock for too short a time for any assimilation
to have taken place. In terms of pronunciation they are 'outsiders',
and to attempt to describe them with the other informants will lead
to unfortunate complications. It will be shown in Chapter V that
there are linguistic grounds for eliminating these four informants
from the statistical tests.

Place of birth and upbringing

The important factor here is not only the actual birthplace, but also
the place where the earliest years of life were spent, since there is
plenty of evidence from psychologists that this is the formative
period. The informants were classified into three groups:

(1) *Born in Cannock Urban District:* 43 informants, $53\frac{3}{4}\%$ of the
total. These are the people for whom the place-code is underlined
in column I of Table 26b. Those who were born outside Cannock
were grouped according to the distance of the birthplace.

(2) *Up to 14 miles from Cannock town centre:* 22 informants, $27\frac{1}{2}\%$ of
the total. This area coincides roughly with South Staffordshire.

(3) *More than 14 miles from Cannock town centre:* 15 informants,
$18\frac{3}{4}\%$ of the total. Of these, four were born less than thirty miles
from Cannock.

This last group includes the four informants who will later be excluded. They are nos. 12, 31, 53 and 75.

Time lived in Cannock

This information is derived from columns I to M of Table 26b. Because of the age-range from 23 to 79, it is expressed as a percentage of the informant's age.

(1) *100%, i.e. whole of life:* 31 informants, 38¾% of the total.

(2) *50% to 99%:* 29 informants, 36¼% of the total.

(3) *Less than 50%:* 20 informants, 25% of the total.

Occupation and social class

We have already observed (page 9) that one does not expect dustmen and bank managers to speak in the same way, even if they are both locally born. Several other pairs of occupations could easily have been chosen to illustrate this point. This is where we have to deal with the controversial question of *class*, with all its political overtones. In Cannock, the very uttering of this word places a speaker in a social group, since both /klɑːs/ and /klæs/ pronunciations are to be heard—and the use of 'long A' (as it is called) by some is as much a class-signal as the dropping of H by others.

In a precise, scientific, survey of this kind, it would have been useless to try to work with vague terms like 'upper middle class', 'working class' and so forth. No two people agree in their use of such expressions, which for too long have been used merely as insults or slogans in the 'class war', and thus emptied of any meaning they might otherwise have had. We require a neutral method of classifying people, without emotional overtones.

Government departments make use of two official classifications, both based on occupation, and both taking no account of wealth or birth. One of these schemes classifies occupations into seventeen *socio-economic groups.* This scheme was studied in connection with the Cannock survey, and the classification was made, but several of the groups were not represented, and others included only a few informants. Socio-economic grouping turned out to be too fine in some places and too crude in others; it also overlapped considerably with the other scheme of classification which was adopted for the survey.

The second scheme classifies people, by occupation only, into five *social classes*, as follows:

Class I (*professional*): those occupations for which a university degree is a normal entrance requirement, e.g. doctors, university lecturers. By an exception, all parochial clergy are placed in this class, whether they are graduates or not.

Class II (*intermediate*): occupations not requiring a degree as a necessity, but which demand professional training, e.g. school-teachers, nurses.

Class III (*skilled*): This class is subdivided into manual (e.g. miners, bricklayers) and non-manual (e.g. shop assistants) sections.

Class IV (*semi-skilled*): also subdivided into manual (e.g. farm labourers) and non-manual (e.g. domestic service) sections.

Class V (*unskilled*): e.g. lavatory attendants.

Since Classes III and IV are subdivided this scheme provides a sevenfold classification. It so happens that in the random sample of the Cannock electorate there are no representatives of Classes I or V. This is a useful reminder that random samples are not infallible. One would not conclude that there are no professional or unskilled workers in the Urban District, no doctors or no dustmen—only that such people form an insignificantly small proportion of the population. Effectively, therefore, we have a fivefold classification of our informants.

The following table places each informant into his or her social class, the letters M and N indicating manual and non-manual respectively. There is also a list of all the informant's occupations, in chronological order. In each case the current occupation (or most recent occupation in the case of retired people and married women who have given up work) is placed last, and this is used for determining social class.

TABLE 3

Informant Number	Social Class	Occupations
1.	IIIM	bakery work; housewife.
3.	IIIN	factories; offices; shops; housewife.
4.	IIIM	bricklayer.
5.	IIIM	painter and decorator.
7.	IVM	machinist in clothing factory.
8.	IVN	domestic service; housewife.
9.	IVM	builder's labourer.

TABLE 3 (*cont.*)

Informant Number	Social Class	Occupations
10.	IVN	domestic service; housewife.
11.	IIIM	domestic service; fitter for National Coal Board.
12.	IVM	machinist in factory; housewife.
13.	IIIM	miner; retired.
14.	IIIN	shop assistant; housewife.
15.	IIIN	regular army; forecourt attendant at petrol station.
16.	IIIN	clerical official to Cannock Urban District Council.
18.	IIIN	accounts clerk; housewife.
19.	IVM	pipelayer (civil engineering).
20.	IIIM	foreman bricklayer.
21.	IVN	policeman (in Israel); traffic warden.
22.	IIIM	mechanic in mine.
23.	IIIN	shorthand-typist; housewife.
25.	IIIN	clerical official for National Coal Board.
26.	IIIM	winding engineer in mine.
28.	II	nurse; housewife.
29.	II	company director.
30.	IIIM	miner.
31.	IIIM	deputy in mine.
33.	IIIM	miner; retired.
34.	IVM	service labourer (car accessories).
35.	II	chemist.
36.	IVM	roof-tiler.
37.	IVN	domestic service; assistant laundress in old peoples' home; housewife.
38.	IIIM	domestic service; various jobs in factories; housewife.
39.	IVM	miner; viewer at ball-bearing factory.
40.	IIIM	builder and bricklayer (own business).
41.	IIIN	clerk.
42.	IVM	machinist (textiles); housewife.
43.	IIIM	butcher (own business).
44.	IIIM	coach-driver; retired.
45.	IIIM	colliery winder.
46.	II	mines rescue superintendent.
48.	IIIM	assistant in bakery.
49.	IIIM	trunk mains, South Staffordshire Water Board.
50.	II	sales manager.
51.	II	optician.
52.	IIIM	housewife.
53.	IIIM	miner.

TABLE 3 (cont.)

Informant Number	Social Class	Occupations
54.	IIIN	clerk; housewife.
55.	IVM	machine operator (tools).
56.	IVN	housewife.
57.	IIIN	sales-woman.
60.	II	housewife.
61.	II	nurse in child welfare; housewife.
62.	IIIM	sign-writer.
63.	IVM	hairdresser.
64.	IVM	automatic press-worker; housewife.
65.	II	nurse; housewife.
66.	IVN	housewife.
67.	IIIN	shop assistant; housewife.
68.	IVN	caterer (own business).
69.	IVM	machine shop inspector.
71.	IIIN	miner; clerical official for National Coal Board.
72.	IIIN	secretary to Surveyor to Stafford Rural District Council.
73.	IVM	fitter's mate.
74.	IIIM	mechanic with National Coal Board.
75.	IIIM	miner.
76.	IIIN	shorthand-typist; housewife.
77.	II	domestic service; mental nurse; housewife.
78.	IIIM	plasterer.
80.	IIIM	carpenter and joiner.
82.	IIIM	foreman (heavy chemicals).
83.	IVN	domestic service; machinist; housewife.
84.	IVM	mains pipelayer (engineering).
85.	IIIM	welder.
86.	IIIM	wharf engineer; long distance haulage; miner; retired.
87.	IVM	farm worker.
88.	IVM	labourer for building firm.
89.	IIIM	engineer.
91.	II	schoolteacher; housewife.
92.	IVN	wholesale grocer (own business).
93.	IVM	packer.

The reader who studies this table may find some anomalies in it, but the definitions are taken from *Classification of Occupations 1966*, issued by the General Register Office in connection with the sample census of that year.

Married women are generally in the same class as their husbands;

this is why those women who have only been housewives are not all in the same class.

The numbers in the five classes represented in Cannock are as follows:

Class II: 11 informants, $13\frac{3}{4}\%$ of the total.

Class III (*non-manual*): 14 informants, $17\frac{1}{2}\%$ of the total.

Class III (*manual*): 29 informants, $36\frac{1}{4}\%$ of the total.

Class IV (*non-manual*): 9 informants, $11\frac{1}{4}\%$ of the total.

Class IV (*manual*): 17 informants, $21\frac{1}{4}\%$ of the total.

CHAPTER III

Some phonological considerations

The small amount of phonological material presented so far has been given, for convenience, in a traditional phonemic transcription. In later chapters a different type of notation will be used; the purpose of this chapter is to explain why this has been done and the nature of the transcription employed; it is not intended to be a closely argued discussion of phonological theory, which would be inappropriate here.

The concept of the *phoneme* as distinct from a *phone* or speech-sound has been in use for the best part of a century. Various definitions have been propounded, differing widely in formulation. For example, there is the definition given by Daniel Jones in *The Phoneme: its Nature and Use*:

> a family of sounds in a given language which are related in character and are used in such a way that no one member ever occurs in a word in the same phonetic context as any other member. (page 10.)

This may be contrasted with Bloomfield's idea of the phoneme as those features which are common to all its allophones:

> These distinctive features occur in lumps or bundles, each one of which we call a phoneme. (*Language*, page 79.)

In many ways these definitions are opposites, and yet most linguists have handled their material on similar lines, the most rigorous approach being that of American structuralists in the period following the Second World War and before the rise of generative phonology. The basic assumption of this kind of phonemics is that the phonological analysis is the first stage of a linguistic description, on which the grammar is subsequently built; to avoid circularity, therefore, no grammatical information may be included in the phonology. In particular, three requirements emerged as essential: *linearity, invariance* and *bi-uniqueness*. These are discussed briefly below; for more details the reader can consult Noam Chomsky's highly critical account in *Current Issues in Linguistic Theory*, pages 78ff.

(1) *Linearity*. To each sound in the speech-chain there must correspond a single phoneme in the same position in the phonemic transcription. As a general principle this works very well, but consider the French nasal vowels: the occurrence of these, rather than a corresponding oral vowel, is entirely predictable by simple rules which make no appeal to grammar. The French phoneme inventory could be reduced by four if the nasal vowels could be regarded as realisations of oral vowels plus nasal consonant when followed by another consonant or pause; but the linearity condition does not permit this.

(2) *Invariance*. Whenever a sound occurs, it must always be the realisation of the same phoneme. As in the linearity case, this is all very well as a general principle, but sometimes it leads to more complex descriptions. In Classical Latin, as in many languages, the velar nasal [ŋ] only occurred before velar stops (*ancora, sanguis*). It seems probable that G before N was also pronounced as a velar nasal (W. S. Allen, *Vox Latina*, p. 23). The most natural way of dealing with this situation would be to regard the velar nasal as an allophone of /n/ in *ancora, inquit* and similar words, and as an allophone of /g/ in *agnus, dignus*, etc. In both cases the occurrence of [ŋ] is conditioned by the phonetic context. But the invariance principle does not allow a sound to be an allophone of two different phonemes; and since besides *ng* and *gn* there are also occurrences of *nn* (*annus*) and *gg* (*agger*), the only solution available is to make the velar nasal a phoneme in its own right.

The velar nasal presents similar problems in the Received Pronunciation of English and also in the 'Cannock accent'. In RP it forms distinctive contrasts with /n/ in some positions (*sin—sing*) whereas in others it is contextually conditioned (*ink*). In the system used in this book, [ŋ] will be regarded as an allophone of /n/ in the second case, and as a realisation of the phoneme sequence /ng/ in the first; but in terms of autonomous phonemics this would be contrary to both the linearity and invariance principles.

(3) *Bi-uniqueness*. This is probably the most important principle: given a phonemic transcription, there must be only one possible way of interpreting it phonetically; conversely, given a speech-chain, there must be only one way of transcribing it phonemically. In other words, there must be a strict one-to-one correspondence between the two levels. If the linearity and invariance conditions are adhered to, the bi-uniqueness condition will in most cases be satisfied.

The object of Chomsky's discussion of this subject is to show that when these principles are rigorously applied, phonemics becomes unworkable, and that it has only been made practicable by 'bending the rules'. According to Erik Fudge (introduction to *Phonology*, pp. 10–11) the problem arises from the use of the speech-sound as the basis and then expanding the description to cover wider groupings, syllables, morphemes, words, etc.:

> It is awkward, not to say theoretically inconsistent, to refer to morphological and other grammatical facts in the treatment of phonemic structure. (. . .) All linguists have agreed that a particular phonemic representation can have associated with it just *one* phonetic representation except that optional pronunciations (*free variants*) are permissible in appropriate instances. But working in the 'discovery' order means that phonetic form determines phonemic form, therefore the converse of this should also be required, i.e. that each phonetic form can have associated with it just *one* phonemic form: this is the requirement which Chomsky calls *bi-uniqueness*. (. . .) This would rule out such possibilities as assigning to German [bunt] the phonemic /bunt/ when it represents the root *bunt* 'coloured' and the form /bund/ when it represents the root *Bund* 'treaty' (which has inflected forms [bundəs], etc.)—this simplifies the morphology, and gives the correct pronunciation, if we have a rule stating that final voiced plosives become voiceless.

It is important to realise that these objections, which are perfectly valid, are not objections to traditional phonemics as such, but only to one particularly rigorist interpretation of the theory. At an earlier period, some linguists were much more flexible in their approach: Sapir, for example, was prepared, where necessary, to appeal to morphological patterning, and his treatment of the English velar nasal flouts the linearity condition:

A second example is ŋ of *sing*. In spite of what phoneticians tell us about this sound (*b:m* as *d:n* as *g:*ŋ), no naïve English-speaking person can be made to feel in his bones that it belongs to a single series with *m* and *n*. Psychologically it cannot be grouped with them because, unlike them, it is not a freely moveable consonant (there are no words beginning with ŋ). It still *feels* like ŋg, however little it sounds like it. The relation *ant: and* = *sink: sing* is psychologically as well as historically correct. Orthography is by no means solely responsible for the '*ng* feeling' of ŋ. (E. Sapir: 'Sound Patterns in Language', in *Phonology*, p. 111.)

If phonology is the foundation-stone of a linguistic description, then to allow grammatical considerations to have weight at this stage, as Sapir does, certainly runs the risk of circularity. But there is another approach: it is possible to begin the description with the largest units (sentences) and to work from these to smaller units. This order of description, which is used both in tagmemics and in generative grammar, bases itself on the syntax; phonology is a later stage, and is legitimately dependent on the syntax.

Generative grammar, however, does not merely reverse the order of working in phonology—it abandons traditional phonemics entirely and adopts a new approach to phonology. This was sketched out by Chomsky in *Current Issues in Linguistic Theory* and has since been developed by other workers. The generative approach to phonology is presented in detail in its application to English in Chomsky and Halle's *The Sound Pattern of English*; an application of the theory to French can be found in *French Phonology and Morphology* by Sanford A. Schane.

Generative phonology starts with the strings of formatives which make up the output of the syntactic component of the grammar. These include abstract morphemes such as 'past', 'accusative singular', etc., and *readjustment rules* are required to convert these to the level of *systematic phonemics*, which is the input to the phonological component. Phonological rules convert this representation to a level of *systematic phonetics*. This is all done in terms of *distinctive features*; phonemic and phonetic symbols are merely convenient cover symbols for bundles of features.

The input to the phonological component, the systematic phonemic level, is not to be identified with a traditional phonemic transcription. This upper level includes units which would have been called morphophonemes by American structuralists. One gains the impression that Chomsky and Halle's phonological component deals primarily with details of morphology. This impression is confirmed by the output of the component which looks remarkably like a traditional *phonemic* transcription. In fact one looks in vain for any reference to the occurrence of clear and dark /l/, the degree of aspiration of voiceless stops, and other matters which would be expected in a phonetic transcription. To be fair, there is no claim that the phonetic matrices are complete, and irrelevant details are stated to be omitted, but the variation between clear and dark /l/ is one of the most noticeable allophonic features of English and can scarcely be dismissed as irrelevant.

Schane's work on French illustrates the same point: his output is overtly a phonemic transcription, and is enclosed in slant lines, not square brackets. His 'phonological' rules deal in the main with *morphological* alternations within French (e.g. *vouloir—veulent—volonté*). This type of description is useful and provides insights into the morphological and morphophonemic workings of the languages concerned; but it is not phonology as traditionally understood.

We can only conclude that 'phonology' in generative grammar means something different from what it has been generally understood to mean, and that the success of the generative approach to morphophonemic problems does not invalidate the phonemic principle. Indeed the relaxation of the linearity, invariance and bi-uniqueness principles, together with the inverted order of linguistic description, seem to have strengthened the phoneme theory, rather than weakened it.

Nevertheless, Chomsky's criticisms of autonomous phonemics remain quite valid, and must be dealt with. But although we may grant that the phonemic theory in its extreme form is unworkable, this does not seem to be a reason for abandoning a hypothesis which is intuitively satisfying and has achieved many useful results.

In this connection we may remember that there has frequently been a link between phonemics and the provision of an orthography for hitherto unwritten languages. The sub-title of Kenneth L. Pike's *Phonemics* is 'a technique for reducing languages to writing'. This link has led to the accusation that phonemics is a hypostatisation of the Roman alphabet, but this is not necessarily an objection, since the alphabet as originally conceived by the Phoenicians and Greeks seems to have been based on an unconscious acknowledgement of the phoneme as the minimal unit. Now in many languages, notably English and French, the traditional orthography bears little resemblance to the phonemic transcription devised by linguists. At one time, this was assumed to be evidence of inadequacy in the conventional spelling. Closer examination, however, suggests that the orthography may emphasize certain regularities in the language that the orthodox phonemic transcription obscures. In English, for example, certain vowels are regularly reduced to [ə] in unstressed positions; in French, certain vowels and consonants are obligatorily deleted in particular contexts (*elizion* and *liaison*, which Schane links together under the label *truncation*). In neither language does the orthography take note of these changes; nevertheless they are readily supplied in pronunciation because the conditioning factors involved are entirely phonological (in the strict sense of that word). In spite of what has been said above about generative 'phonology', there does seem to be a case for re-defining the phoneme to take into account phenomena of this type; provided that only phonological conditioning is admitted.

Transcriptions of this kind are not new: they are usually called morphophonemic and have been treated with suspicion in the past because they necessarily flout the conditions of linearity, invariance and bi-uniqueness. In Latin, for instance, the stem *reg-* appears with a voiceless stop in the nominative *rēx*; the conditioning is purely phonological (assimilation to a following voiceless /s/); but André Martinet is unwilling to generalise the stem throughout the paradigm:

> In any case, it is clear that to adopt transcriptions like . . . /rēgs/, /rēgis/ is to sacrifice the results of the phonological analysis in order to simplify the presentation of the meaningful unit s. . . (Martinet: 'De la morphonologie', in *Phonology*, p. 94.)

He then refers to 'certain automatic alternations', using nasalisation in French as an example, and says:

> It is clear that this kind of automatic process has nothing in common with the kind which, entirely conditioned by the phonic context, results in the choice of a particular phoneme variant . . . (Ibid., p. 97.)

Surely, if the alternation is indeed entirely conditioned by the phonic context, it is legitimate to ignore it in transcription, leaving the actual pronunciation to be ascertained by phonetic rules, as French spelling in fact does? It may be necessary to refer to the position of word- and morpheme-boundaries, but this is permissible in the 'reductive order' of description; and rigorously autonomous phonemics never succeeded in avoiding this anyway.

Orthographic considerations therefore suggest that there is a case to be made out for an *abstract phonemic transcription* which is different both from an autonomous phonemic transcription and from the lexical input to the 'phonological' component of a generative grammar. A further pointer to its possible validity arises from a theory put forward more than a quarter of a century ago by Martin Joos (in *Acoustic Phonetics*, especially Chapter 5). He suggested there that the phoneme is a completely abstract entity existing in the mind of speaker and listener. To each phoneme, there correspond one or more *neuremes*; in the case of speech-production, these are to be understood as units of 'instructions' from the central nervous system to the organs of speech. These neuremes would be bundles of features —articulatory features, since they regulate the movement of the tongue, vocal cords, etc. It would also seem to be necessary to postulate the existence of neuremes consisting of bundles of acoustic or perceptual features, to account for the process of speech-recognition. Since it appears that much of the fine detail of articulatory phonetic processes is lost in transmission, we could expect no one-to-one correspondence between acoustic and articulatory neuremes.

In terms of generative grammar, it is the lowest-level phonetic output that gives 'instructions' to the speech apparatus. Joos' neuremes, on the other hand, are one step removed from phonetic reality, since they are assumed to be modified by physical constraints. But this is a mere detail; the point is that this hypothesis makes the phoneme a much more abstract notion than it is usually taken to be in autonomous phonemics; it has to be associated with two sets of neuremes, one articulatory, the other acoustic; and since there can be no bi-uniqueness relationship between the latter, it seems plausible that the phoneme can be liberated from this requirement also.

Whether an abstract phonemic transcription is of any use or interest may well depend on the language in question. In Classical Latin there are no great differences between an abstract phonemic transcription, an autonomous phonemic transcription, a narrow phonetic transcription, and the conventional spelling. In French, autonomous phonemic and narrow phonetic transcriptions are very similar, since this is a language with very little allophonic variation; but an abstract phonemic transcription resembles the conventional spelling in many respects, since both are to be interpreted in terms of the purely phonological rules (about elision, liaison and nasalisation) that native French speakers have to apply when reading aloud.

To return to English, there are similarities between an abstract phonemic transcription and traditional orthography. But English spelling is a less useful guide than French: French spelling is fairly consistent from writing to sound, though not vice versa; English spelling is inconsistent in both directions.

It may seem perverse to indulge in this theoretical excursus in a piece of socio-linguistic research. But it was the research material itself that suggested a substitute for autonomous phonemics, for the following reasons:

Although the bulk of the informants in the random sample were native to Cannock, or at least to the South Staffordshire area, there were others who came from different parts of the country. Consequently a wide variety of accents of English were represented. A need emerged for a common framework in which they could all be described in phonological terms. Obviously, major projects like the *Survey of English Dialects* have handled far more disparate material than that to be found in the Cannock survey, but the interests in that case were phonetic, not phonological. Even so, there have been studies of restricted areas that have made use of the conventional phonemicisation of English. One such study is R. A. Bowyer's *A Study of Social Accents in a South London Suburb*, a survey which uses a similar sampling technique and the same statistical tests as those used here. Bowyer refers to the thesis which originally reported on the Cannock survey, but presents his results in a more conventional manner. There are two reasons, it appears, why the conventional phonemic transcription is adequate in his case:

(1) Bowyer sorts his informants into two groups according to their geographical provenance: those who were born and had lived all their lives in Beckenham, together with those whose accents shared the same regional basis, formed Group 1, while those whose accents had different regional origins formed Group 2. The detailed phonetic and phonemic study was carried out only with Group 1 informants. As a result there is less variation in the material than in the Cannock survey.

(2) The informants in the Cannock survey were each compared, in terms of pronunciation, with two extremes: the Received Pronunciation (RP) and a basic 'Cannock accent' which is described in the next chapter. Bowyer uses a similar approach: his extremes are RP and Cockney, as described by Sivertsen, op. cit. He regards Cockney as the extreme regional form, and RP as a more neutral, non-regional variety (op. cit., pp. 8 and 13). This is no doubt true for a South London suburb and reduces the amount of variation between speakers, but it is not possible to agree that RP is non-regional, nor even that it is accepted as standard in the Midlands and the North. We may grant that it is the prestige dialect of the whole country, and that its prestige is increasing with the influence of mass-communication. That there is strong RP influence on some varieties of Cannock speech will become evident in the following pages; but it is not the only factor.

An abstract transcription was used in the Cannock survey in order to provide a phonemic system which would be common to as many informants as possible. Specific pronunciations could then be treated as realisations at the phonetic level of the abstract phonemes. In spite of the broader framework, there are still cases of phonemic differences between speakers, especially in the treatment of complex vowel nuclei, but the abstract transcription ensures that only major differences show up at the phonemic level. The patterning of the velar nasal is an example of this. In the original version of this study, it was assumed that there was a contrast of phonemes in RP between *singer* and *finger*, but not in the 'Cannock accent'. But this was an assumption derived from autonomous phonemics, which requires a /ŋ/ phoneme in RP. It is now realised that this analysis is incorrect (cf. the quotation from Sapir, p. 31 above) because it overemphasises the difference between systems. In fact there is no velar nasal abstract phoneme in any variety of English, only differences in the rules for realising the NG sequence at the phonetic level.

Abstract phonemics will be used in the remainder of this book. For *phonetic* transcriptions the usual IPA symbols and diacritics are used and enclosed in square brackets. *Abstract phonemic* transcriptions will be enclosed in slant lines, but to show that they are different from autonomous phonemes and from phonetic realities, a different symbolisation will be used. The symbols will be printed in upper case characters, and as far as possible the conventions of English spelling will be adopted. Thus /L/ will be used for the initial phoneme of *lap*, /P/ for that of *pin*, etc. Digraphs are sometimes needed: the second element is printed in lower case, and the whole is a symbol for a *single* phoneme, e.g. /Ch/ represents the initial and final phonemes of *church*, and /Oi/ and /Ou/ the vowels of *boy* and *bough*. The only diacritic used is the macron, to increase the number of available vowel-symbols. Symbols for the vowels have been chosen in order to illuminate alternations such as *divIde—divIsion* or *nAtion—nAtional*. (This is explained in more detail in the next chapter.) Logically, this is unnecessary, but it has two practical advantages: it simplifies morphological description (though we are not concerned with that here), and it is easier to read.

The conditions of linearity, invariance and bi-uniqueness do not apply to an abstract transcription. For example, the labiodental nasal [ɱ] can quite properly be considered an allophone of both /M/ and /N/, and a phoneme sequence such as /AR/ can be realised as a single vowel. The vowel [ə], which in autonomous phonemics has to be a separate phoneme although it only occurs in unstressed syllables, is here taken to be an unstressed realisation of several vowel phonemes.

Abstract phonemic transcriptions are converted to sound by the application of rules which are either unconditional (e.g. /Th/ is always realised as [θ]) or dependent for their operation on the phonological context only (e.g. /H/ may be realised as [ɦ] in intervocalic position). It is permissible to refer to word- and morpheme-boundaries where necessary. It would be beyond the scope of this research to discuss in any detail the nature of the realisation rules: since in the following pages whole words are only rarely given in transcription, these questions can be ignored for our purposes. An informal statement of phonetic realisations for RP will be found on pages 39–47; since the rules involved are in principle the same as those used in reading aloud any passage of English, the reader should have no difficulty in interpreting the transcriptions.

CHAPTER IV

The two extremes

It is mentioned on page 22 that the varieties of pronunciation found among the eighty informants range from approximations to the Received Pronunciation at one end of the scale to what we may term a 'Cannock accent' at the other. We shall now try to establish what are the distinguishing features of speech at each end of the scale, and then describe the speech of all eighty informants in terms of these two extremes.

The Received Pronunciation (RP) has been fully described in many places; readers who want more details than are given in this book should consult *An Outline of English Phonetics* by Daniel Jones or *An Introduction to the Pronunciation of English* by A. C. Gimson.

RP is not the speech of any single person; it is an abstraction, based on features of pronunciation common to a large number of speakers. At the opposite end of our scale of pronunciation we need to establish a system for the 'broadest' accent of Cannock Urban District. From now on we will refer to this 'Cannock accent' as CUD for short, and we will base it on the speech of a number of suitable informants.

Only a minority of the informants in the survey were suitable for establishing the nature of CUD. They had to have been born within the urban district and to have never lived outside it, not even in Huntington or Great Wyrley or any other of the adjoining parishes. But this is not a sufficient qualification to guard against possible outside influences, and it was clearly necessary to impose two further restrictions: the informant's mother had to be a native of Staffordshire (since an infant normally learns its language first of all from its mother, and can therefore be considerably influenced by her speech-habits); and the informant had to have left school as soon as the law permitted at the time, because CUD has no prestige whatever and education has been known to obliterate it.

There were twenty-five informants who fulfilled these requirements: nos. 1, 4, 5, 7, 13, 14, 19, 20, 22, 23, 33, 36, 40, 44, 45,49, 52, 54, 66, 67, 73, 76, 78, 80 and 85. Those features of pronunciation which are shared by all or most of these informants form part of the CUD system which is described later in this chapter.

There now follows a brief description of RP in terms of the abstract phonemics explained in the previous chapter.

The Received Pronunciation (RP)

RP English has thirty-seven abstract phonemes. They can be classi-fied as *vowels*, which normally function as the nucleus of a syllable, or as *consonants*, which do not.

Vowels: /Ā/, /A/, /Ē/, /E/, /Ī/, /I/, /Ō/, /O/, /Oi/, /Ou/,/Q̄/,/Q/, /Ū/, /U/. (14)

Consonants: /B/, /C/, /Ch/, /D/, /Dh/, /F/, /G/, /H/, /J/, /L/, /M/, /N/, /P/, /R/, /S/, /Sh/, /T/, /Th/, /V/, /W/, /Y/, /Z/, /Zh/. (23)

For reasons given in the previous chapter, purely phonetic criteria would be inappropriate in further classifying phonemes at this level of abstraction; instead, our classification will be based on the ways in which the phonemes form patterns in English grammar.

The vowels. The choice of symbols to represent the vowels already anticipates the results of the following paragraphs. At the phonetic level, the usual symbols of the International Phonetic Association will be used, enclosed in square brackets.

Phonetically, RP English has pure vowels, diphthongs and some speakers have triphthongs. We shall treat the diphthongs as single phonemes, since they alternate with the pure vowels in three ways:

(1) When a speaker of RP recites the alphabet, the vowels A, E, I, O and U are pronounced, respectively:

[ẹι] [ui] [äι] [əɷ] [jü].

(2) Next we consider the effect on pronunciation of adding a mute E to certain short words containing a pure vowel. This process gives the following alternations, which confirm the results obtained by considering the vowels in isolation:

TABLE 4a

	Pure vowel	Diphthong	
mat	[æ]	[ęɪ]	mate
pet	[ę]	[ui]	Pete
sit	[ɪ]	[äɪ]	site
not	[ɒ]	[əꭥ]	note
cut	[ɐ]	[jü]	cute

(3) Lastly, there are morphological alternations between different forms of the same basic word, as exemplified in these pairs (the vowel under consideration is printed in capitals):

TABLE 4b

	Pure vowel	Diphthong	
nAtional	[æ]	[ęɪ]	nAtion
serEnity	[ę]	[ui]	serEne
divIsion	[ɪ]	[äɪ]	divIde
cOnic	[ɒ]	[əꭥ]	cOne
abUndance	[ɐ]	[äꭥ]	abOUnd

These alternations, which are such a feature of Modern English, have not always been part of the language. In Middle English (i.e. as spoken between roughly 1100 and 1500), words like these had a contrast between long and short vowels. The present patterns are the result of a complex series of changes of vowel quality in which the long vowels became diphthongs; the process appears to have extended over the period 1450 to 1700, and is known as the Great Vowel Shift. This historical example leads to the same result except in the last case (*abundance—abound*). Alternations like this one are rare (*profundity—profound* is another example) and seem to be confined to words of Norman-French or Latin origin.

The grounds for assigning phonemic symbols to the vowels should now be clear. The symbols /A/, /E/, /I/, /O/ and /U/ are assigned to the short vowels of *mat, pet, sit, not* and *cut* respectively. The corresponding diphthong in the three alternation patterns is given the same symbol with a macron over it. Since the alternation between *cut* and *cute* is a much more frequent type than that between *abundance* and *abound*, the symbol /Ū/ is used to represent [jü]. This also accords more closely with English spelling conventions. The diphthong [ɑꭥ] which is still pronounced [uː] in some dialects of Northern England and Southern Scotland, is given the compound symbol /Ou/.

The vowel /Ō/, as in *boat*, is derived from Middle English [ɔː].

Middle English had another long O-like vowel [o:]. This has become the diphthong [ou] as in *boot*. Similarly, the vowel /U/, as in *cut*, is derived from Middle English [ʊ]. In some words, for reasons which are not entirely clear, this vowel has remained unchanged: examples are *bush, cushion, pull*. We give this short vowel the symbol /Q/ (which is a 'spare' letter not needed for the consonants) and regard [ou] as its diphthongal equivalent /Q̄/. This is merely done for convenience since there are no alternations between these two phonemes, though they may both be represented in English spelling by the letters OO: *book, food*.

The diphthong [ɔɪ], phonemic symbol /Oi/, has no alternations and, as will become clear in the following paragraphs, allows none of the modifications which apply to the other phonemes. Most of the words in which it occurs are of Norman-French origin and came into the language in the Middle English period; it was unaffected by the Great Vowel Shift. Even now it seems not to have been integrated into the English vowel system: a glance at Vowel Chart 1 (page 42) shows that it spoils the symmetry of the pattern.

In the following account of RP vowels, the reader should bear in mind that all short vowels, apart from /I/ and /Q/ are pronounced [ə] in unstressed syllables.

We classify the vowel phonemes as follows: English RP has eight *base vowel phonemes*, all realised phonetically as diphthongs with finishing points in the close front or close back region. They are shown here in Table 5, with the main allophone and an example of each, and also in Vowel Chart 1.

TABLE 5

RP base phoneme	Main Allophone	Example
/Ā/	[ęɪ]	*may*
/Ē/	[úi]	*me*
/Ī/	[äɪ]	*sigh*
/Ou/	[äω]	*how*
/Q̄/	]ʊu]	*boo*
/Ō/	[əω]	*toe*
/Ū/	[jü]	*cue*
/Oi/	[ɔɪ]	*boy*

Vowel Chart 1—RP base vowels

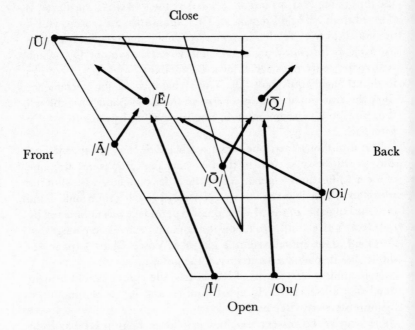

Corresponding to these is a set of what may loosely be called 'short' phonemes, realised phonetically as pure short vowels. They are shown in Table 6 and Vowel Chart 2.

TABLE 6

Base	'Short' phoneme	Main allophone	Example
/Ā/	/A/	[æ]	*rap*
/Ē/	/E/	[ɛ]	*met*
/Ī/	/I/	[ɪ]	*knit*
/Ou/	/U/	[ɐ]	*rut*
/Q̄/	/Q/	[ʊ]	*put*
/Ō/	/O/	[ɒ]	*tot*
/Ū/	none		
/Oi/	none		

Vowel Chart 2—RP 'short' vowels

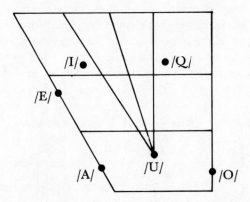

These 'short' phonemes can be further modified by the addition of /R/. These combinations of pure vowel + /R/ are realised phonetically as pure vowels, but they are always longer than the corresponding 'short' vowel occurring in the same environment. For example, compare *bat* with *Bart* and *bad* with *bard*. In these combinations the /R/ has no consonantal value; the words involved are mostly those that had post-vocalic /r/ in an earlier stage of the language, but also some that have never had it, like *father, calm, shawl*. Some English dialects still have post-vocalic /r/, as does most American speech, but the Cannock system does not, so there can be no confusion in using it. The symbol /H/ is available also, and would have to be used in those dialects which still retain post-vocalic /r/, but /R/ is preferred here for historical reasons. The effect of /R/ on the 'short' phonemes is shown in Table 7 and Vowel Chart 3.

TABLE 7

Base	'Short'	'Short' + /R/	Main allophone	Example
/Ā/	/A/	/AR/	[ä:]	*mar*
/Ē/	/E/ —	/ER/ ⎫		⎧ *merge*
/Ī/	/I/ —	/IR/ ⎬	[ə:]	⎨ *sir*
/Ou/	/U/ —	/UR/ ⎭		⎩ *cur*
/Q̄/	/Q/	none		
/Ō/	/O/	/OR/	[ɔ:]	*tor*
/Ū/	none			
/Oi/	none			

The number of contrasts is reduced: three phoneme sequences /ER/, /IR/, /UR/, have the same realisation [ə:].

Finally, there exist also combinations of the base vowel phonemes with /R/. In this case the phonetic realisations are centring diphthongs or triphthongs. Note that the whole diphthong is a realisation of a sequence of phonemes; the central vowel is not an additional allophone of /R/. These sounds are shown in Table 8 and Vowel Chart 3.

TABLE 8

Base	Base + /R/	Main Allophone	Example
/Ā/	/ĀR/	[ɛə]	*mare*
/Ĕ/	/ĔR/	[ɪə]	*mere*
/Ĭ/	/ĬR/	[äə]/[äɪə]	*sire*
/Ou/	/OuR/	[ȁə]/[ȁɔə]	*hour*
/Q̱/	/Q̱R/	[ωə]	*boor*
/Ō/	/ŌR/	[ɔə]	*tore*
/Ū/	/ŪR/	[jüə]	*cure*
/Oi/	none		

This sub-system is not really as neat as it seems and is much less stable than the others, as many RP speakers have no /ŌR/ and use /OR/ instead (pronouncing *tore* as *tor*); others use /OR/ in place of /Q̱R/ (pronouncing *boor* as *bore*); still others use /OR/ for all three.

Vowel Chart 3 shows both series of vowels + /R/.

Vowel Chart 3—RP Combinations with /R/.

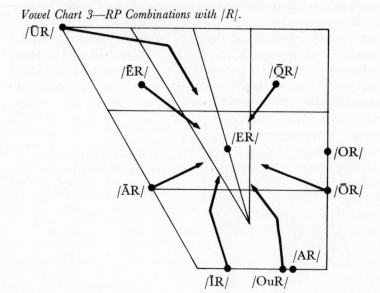

The consonants. It is more difficult to classify the consonants using patterns like those we have established for the vowels. There are a few alternations we can use, e.g. *wife—wives* and similar pairs point to a link between /F/ and /V/, where there is also an obvious phonetic similarity. On the other hand a group like *electric—electricity—electrician* indicates a connection between /C/, /S/ and /Sh/ which is counter-phonetic. A detailed study of such patterns would be out of place in this book; they are studied in section 6 of Eric Fudge's article *On the Nature of Phonological Primes*.

Table 9, which charts the consonants, uses patterns of alternation, supplemented by phonetic considerations.

TABLE 9

	Column (a)	Column (b)	Column (c)	Column (d)
Row *1a*	/M/	– – – – –	/N/	– – – – –
Row *1b(i)*	/P/	/T/	/Ch/	/C/
Row *1b(ii)*	/B/	/D/	/J/	/G/
Row *2(i)*	/F/	/Th/	/Sh/	/S/
Ro. *2(ii)*	/V/	/Dh/	/Zh/	/Z/
Row *3*	/W/	/L/	/Y/	/R/
Row *4*	– – – – – – – –	/H/	– – – – – – – –	

The phonemes in Row 1 are stops, in Row 2 fricatives, in Row 3 a mixture of laterals, frictionless continuants and semivowels (for which we may use the traditional cover-term *liquids*). Row 4 contains only the glottal aspiration /H/. The splitting of Row 1 separates the nasals (1a) from the true stops (*plosives*), though /Ch/ and /J/ are phonetically affricates which behave as single phonemes. The distinction between Rows 1b and 2 is not voicelessness as opposed to voice, since /B/ (for example) is often only fully voiced between vowels; the phonemes in Rows 1b(i) and 2(i) are realised with greater breath-force (*fortis*) than those in Rows 1b(ii) and 2(ii) (*lenis*).

The phonemes in Column (a) are bilabial or labiodental; in Column (b) alveolar or dental; in Column (c) palato-alveolar or palatal. Column (d) includes such phonetically disparate types as velars (/C/, /G/) and alveolars (/S/, /Z/, /R/); the grounds for this grouping can be found in Fudge's article referred to above.

The RP pronunciation of these consonant phonemes is given in the following table. The allophones are merely listed here; for details the reader should consult the handbooks by Jones and Gimson mentioned at the beginning of this chapter.

TABLE 10

RP phoneme	Main allophone	Other allophones
/M/	[m̥]	[m̥] [m̩] [m̩]
/N/	[n]	[ŋ̍] [m̩] [n̩] [ŋ] [n̪]
/P/	[pʻ]	[p]
/T/	[tʻ]	[t] [t̪] [t̬]
/Ch/	[tʃ]	—
/C/	[kʻ]	[k] [k̟ʻ] [k̟]
/B/	[b]	[b]
/D/	[d̪]	[d] [d̪]
/J/	[d̠ʒ̊]	[dʒ]
/G/	[g̊]	[g] [g̊] [g] zero
/F/	[f]	—
/Th/	[θ]	—
/Sh/	[ʃ]	—
/S/	[s]	—
/V/	[v̥]	[v]
/Dh/	[ð̥]	[ð]
/Zh/	[ʒ̊]	[ʒ]
/Z/	[z̥]	[z]
/W/	[w̥]	[w]
/L/	[l]	[ɫ] [l̩] [ɫ̩] [ɫ]
/Y/	[j]	[j̊]
/R/	[ɹ]	[ɹ̥] [ɾ]
/H/	[h]	[ɦ]

The following points call for comment:

/H/. The phoneme sequence /HŪ/ is generally realised as [çü], the palatal fricative [ç] corresponding to both the /H/ and the first part of the diphthong. So *huge* is transcribed /HŪJ/.

The velar nasal [ŋ]. This is taken to be an allophone of /N/ in words like *sink* (/SINC/) where its occurrence is conditioned by the following velar /C/, but in *sing* (/SING/) it is a realisation of the phoneme sequence /NG/ and contrasts with /N/ in *sin*. In this analysis, the velar nasal is not considered to be an autonomous phoneme; the rule required for RP is that /NG/ is realised as [ŋ] before a morphological boundary (either word or morpheme). This restriction prevents the rule from applying in *finger*, where the /G/ is pronounced, but allows it to operate in *singer*, which can be analysed as the verb *sing* plus the agent suffix *-er*.

Syllabic nasals and laterals are taken to be realisations of vowel + nasal or vowel + lateral, e.g. *button* (/BUTON/), *bottle* (/BOTEL/). The phoneme /R/, in addition to patterning as a consonant, also has a place in the description of the vowel system, as we have seen.

The 'Cannock system' (CUD)

As already mentioned, the CUD system is based on the speech of twenty-five of the informants, listed on p. 39. We shall describe it here in contrast with RP; most of the vowels are different, but most of the consonants are similar.

Vowels: /Ā/, /A/, /Ē/, /E/, /Ī/, /I/, /Ō/, /O/, /Oi/, /Ou/, /Q̄/, /Q/, /Ū/. (13, one vowel less than in RP, as CUD has no /U/.)

Consonants: /B/, /C/, /Ch/, /D/, /Dh/, /F/, /G/, /J/, /L/, /M/, /N/, /P/, /R/, /S/, /Sh/, /T/, /Th/, /V/, /W/, /Y/, /Z/, /Zh/. (22, one less than in RP, since CUD has no /H/.)

CUD thus has thirty-five phonemes, compared with thirty-seven in RP.

The vowels. As in RP, CUD has eight base phonemes, all realised phonetically as diphthongs with finishing points in the close front or close back region. Most of the allophones are, however, different from those of RP. They are given here in Table 11 and Vowel Chart 4, which should be compared with Table 5 and Vowel Chart 1 above.

TABLE 11

CUD base phoneme	Main allophone	Example
/Ā/	[εɪ]	*may*
/Ē/	[ʮi]	*me*
/Ī/	[äɪ]	*sigh*
/Ou/	[äɔ]	*how*
/Q̄/	[əü]	*boo*
/Ō/	[ʔɔ]	*toe*
/Ū/	[jü]	*cue*
/Oi/	[ɔɪ]	*boy*

Vowel Chart 4—CUD base vowels

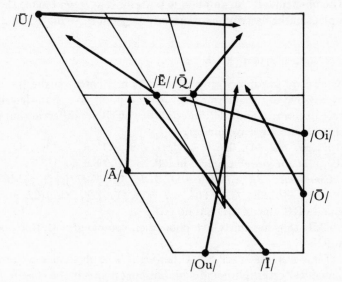

Only /Ū/ has the same pronunciation in RP and CUD.

When we look at the 'short' phonemes, we find that CUD has no contrast between /Q/ and /U/, *cut* and *put* having the same vowel. Table 12 and Vowel Chart 5 should be compared with Table 6 and Vowel Chart 2 above.

TABLE 12

Base	'Short' phoneme	Main allophone	Example
/Ā/	/A/	[a]	*rap*
/Ē/	/E/	[ɛ]	*met*
/Ī/	/I/	[ɪ]	*knit*
/Qu/⎫	/U/⎫	[ɷ]	⎧ *rut*
/Q̃/ ⎭	/Q/ ⎭		⎩ *put*
/Õ/	/O/	[ɒ]	*tot*
/Ū/	none		
/Oi/	none		

Vowel Chart 5—CUD 'short' vowels

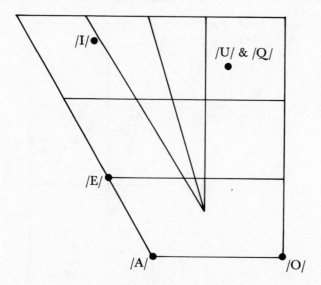

As in RP, these 'short' phonemes can be further modified by the addition of /R/ with very similar results. Table 13 and Vowel Chart 6 should be compared with Table 7 and Vowel Chart 3 above.

TABLE 13

Base	'Short'	'Short' + /R/	Main allophone	Example
/A/	/A/	/AR/	[ɑ:]	mar
/E/	/E/ ⎫	/ER/		merge
/Ī/	/I/ ⎬	/IR/	[ə:]	⎧ sir
/Qu/ ⎱	/U/ ⎭	/UR/		⎩ cur
/Q/ ⎰ /Q/		none		
/Ō/	/O/	/OR/	[ɔ:]	tor
/Ū/	none			
/Oi/	none			

Vowel Chart 6—CUD combinations with /R/

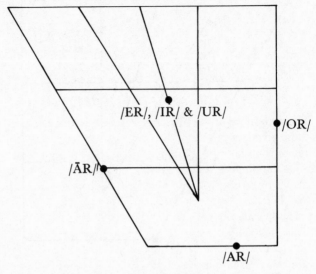

Whereas RP has a set of combinations of the base vowel phonemes with /R/ (Table 8), the situation in CUD is more complex. The only clear example is /ĀR/ as in *mare* which is realised as a pure long vowel [ɛ:]. It is the same type of sound as those in Table 13, and is therefore shown on Vowel Chart 6.

The other combinations of base vowel + /R/ are all realised as a diphthong + [ə]. Unlike their RP counterparts, they clearly form two syllables; also the diphthongal part is in each case identical with the base phoneme (except for /ĀR/), whereas in RP they are different. /ŌR/ does not exist, /OR/ being used instead; that is to say *tore* is always identical with *tor*. We draw the conclusion that in CUD, with the exception of /ĀR/, 'base phoneme + /R/' is not a combination of the RP sort, but a straightforward sequence of phonemes. This means that we must add [ə] to the list of the allophones of /R/.

The consonants. The CUD consonants are listed in Table 14, which is identical with the RP chart in Table 9 above, except for the omission of /H/.

TABLE 14

	Column (a)	Column (b)	Column (c)	Column (d)
Row 1a	/M/	– – – – –	/N/	– – – – –
Row 1b(i)	/P/	/T/	/Ch/	/C/
Row 1b(ii)	/B/	/D/	/J/	/G/
Row 2(i)	/F/	/Th/	/Sh/	/S/
Row 2(ii)	/V/	/Dh/	/Zh/	/Z/
Row 3	/W/	/L/	/Y/	/R/

The definitions of the rows and columns of this table are the same as those given on p. 45.

There is no point in giving a table of CUD consonants with their various allophones, as it would be little different from the RP list in Table 10. We will simply note the points of difference.

/R/. For the reasons already given, it is necessary to add [ə] to the list of 'other allophones'.

/H/. Most of the twenty·five informants used in establishing CUD do in fact use the sound [h], but if we look them up in Appendix II, we find there is no pattern to it. Only a few of these informants did not have an [h] at the beginning of *heel* and *harder*, but there was no consistency in its use. A larger number had no [h] between vowels in *behind*. This is a case where it is important to remember that these words were elicited in isolation, and in many of these cases the additional spontaneous remarks of informants showed examples of 'dropped Hs'. We conclude that when an [h] occurs in CUD it is a case of RP influence on the less prestigious accent, especially as CUD is essentially the speech of the less well educated. CUD we take to be an /H/-less accent under normal conditions.

The nasals. The Cannock system has the phonemes /M/ and /N/ with the same allophonic variations as in RP. The status of the velar nasal [ŋ] is much more problematic. Examine the following table:

TABLE 15

Spelling	RP pronunciation	CUD pronunciation
finger	[fɪŋgə]	[fɪŋgə]
pudding	[pˈʊdɪŋ]	[pˈʊdɪŋ]
sing	[sɪŋ]	[sɪŋg]
singer	[sɪŋə]	[sɪŋgə]
singing	[sɪŋɪŋ]	[sɪŋgɪŋ]

Finger is pronounced in much the same way in both RP and CUD, but the other words are significantly different. We decided (page 46) to take [ŋ] to be an allophone of /N/ when its occurrence is conditioned by a following velar stop, as in *sink*, but otherwise to regard it as the realisation of the phoneme sequence /NG/. We had to place a morphological restriction on the operation of this rule to account for the RP contrast between *singer* and *finger*. In CUD the situation is different: the relevant columns of Table 15 show that velar [ŋ] is always followed by a velar stop, *except after an unstressed vowel*; in other words, to all intents and purposes [ŋ] occurs alone only in the unstressed suffix *-ing*. To account for this we need a rule for the realisation of /NG/, similar to the RP rule, but with a different restriction, namely: /NG/ is realised as [ŋ] in word-final position after unstressed vowels.

The different treatment of /NG/ in RP and CUD is the major difference between the two consonant systems. In the following classification of the differences between RP and CUD it is included, somewhat arbitrarily, among the phonemic differences, although a phonemic transcription alone will not reveal the distinction.

Summary of differences between RP and CUD

There are three types of difference between sound-systems: (1) *phonetic*—the two systems possess the same phoneme with different realisations; (2) *phonemic*—there is a difference in the list of phonemes; (3) *differences of incidence*—the same word may have different sequences of phonemes in the two systems. Applying this distinction to RP and CUD we get the following:

Phonetic differences. Consonants: the same *sounds* occur in RP and CUD, except that CUD does not normally have an [h]. Vowels: most of the vowel-sounds are different, only [jü], [o], [ä:] and [ɔ:] being common to both.

Phonemic differences. (1) RP has an /H/ phoneme, CUD does not; (2) the rule for the realisation of /NG/ is different in the two systems; (3) RP has a contrast between phonemes /U/ and /Q/, CUD has only /Q/; (4) RP has a set of 'base vowel phonemes + /R/', but only one of these /ĀR/, can be be regarded as a combination in CUD; the rest are phoneme sequences.

Differences of incidence. We have not yet looked at these. As a rule, a word containing a given phoneme in RP will have the equivalent phoneme in CUD. See for example the phonemic transcriptions in Table 15 above. There are two discrepancies to be noted:

(1) Normally, words containing /U/ in RP will have /Q/ in CUD, e.g. *rug*, *suck*. There is one exception, but it is a frequent one: the word *one* itself which is /WUN/ in RP and /WON/ in CUD.

(2) Generally, /AR/ in RP corresponds to /AR/ in CUD; they happen to be pronounced alike. Also RP /A/ corresponds to CUD /A/, although these are realised differently ([æ] and [a] respectively). There is a group of words in which RP /AR/ corresponds to CUD /A/: *path*, *glance*, *class*, etc. Historically, none of these words ever had post-vocalic /R/; the change from /A/ to /AR/ is a comparatively recent one in RP (late eighteenth century onwards). Since this is one of the most noticeable differences between RP and the local accents, it is widely imitated by those who wish to 'improve' their speech. Consequently it is not surprising to find it used inconsistently and even in cases where RP does not have it (a phenomenon known as *ultracorrection*)—the writer has heard an /AR/ in *vacuum*.

Ultracorrection is also found among CUD speakers who try to acquire the contrast between /Q/ and /U/. This can result in the use of /U/ in words like *sugar*, *cushion* and *butcher*.

CHAPTER V

A linguistic classification of the informants

The preceding chapter has dealt with the preliminary work that was necessary before the eighty informants could be classified by purely linguistic criteria. We now have comparable descriptions both of the Received Pronunciation and of a basic 'Cannock System' which was abstracted from the speech of twenty-five locally-born informants. The next stage of the analysis was to classify each individual informant by comparing his speech with RP and with CUD.

First, a careful study was made of the points of difference between the RP and CUD systems (they are listed briefly at the end of Chapter IV). The reader will have realised that nearly all the vowels are involved, but only a few of the consonants.

Twenty-three features of pronunciation were studied in making this analysis. In the main they are the features that are different in RP and CUD. The list is given below; each feature has a number and will often be referred to by its number in what follows.

Features of pronunciation

Differences of incidence, i.e. the use of different phonemes in the two systems. There are only two features of this kind:
(1) The vowel of *laugh, dance, glass*: /AR/ in RP; /A/ in CUD.
(2) The vowel of *one*: /U/ in RP; /O/ in CUD.

Phonemic differences, i.e. systematic differences in the phoneme inventory, apart from purely phonetic features. There are four features of this type:
(3) The velar nasal: see Chapter IV, pp. 51–2.

(4) Opposition between /U/ and /Q/: present in RP; absent in CUD, which has only /Q/.

(5) Nature of sequence 'base vowel + /R/': monosyllabic centring diphthongs in RP; in CUD they are disyllabic (except for /ĀR/) and are to be analysed as diphthong + [ə]. Post-vocalic /R/ is phonetically zero in both systems.

(6) The aspirate /H/: present in RP; absent in CUD (see Chapter IV, p. 51 for discussion).

Phonetic differences, i.e. differences only in the realisation of phonemes. There are seventeen features of this type, given in the following table:

TABLE 16

Feature No.		Realisation in RP	Realisation in CUD
(7)	/Ā/	[ęι]	[ει]
(8)	/Ē/	[üi]	[ɪ̈i]
(9)	/Ī/	[äι]	[äι]
(10)	/Ou/	[ä◌]	[ä◌]
(11)	/Q̄/	[◌u]	[əü]
(12)	/Ō/	[ə◌]	[ʔ◌]
(13)	/Oi/	[ɔι]	[ɔι]
(14)	/A/	[æ]	[ä]
(15)	/E/	[ę]	[ε]
(16)	/I/	[ι]	[ι̣]
(17)	/U/	[ɐ]	—
(18)	/Q/	[◌]	[◌]
(19)	/O/	[ɒ]	[ɒ]
(20)	/AR/	[ä:]	[ä:]
(21)	/ER/, /IR/, /UR/	[ə:]	[ə:]
(22)	/OR/	[ɔ:]	[ɔ:]
(23)	/ĀR/	[εə]	[ε:]

The only base vowel not included here is /Ū/, since this has the same realisation [jü], in the speech of all informants. It will be noticed that features 18, 20 and 22 (the vowels /Q/, /AR/ and /OR/) have been included although they have the same realisation in RP and CUD; some informants have realisations of these vowels that are different.

For each of the eighty informants a list was made of the realisations of these twenty-three features. The detailed results are given in the tables of Appendix II. Each feature was marked initially as being (a) the same as in RP or (b) the same as in CUD or (c) different from both. This rough classification then had to be refined by applying a more detailed analysis to the third class of features.

As an example of the method used, consider the phoneme /E/, as occurring in *bet, bed, leg,* etc. The realisation is [ȩ] in RP and [ɛ] in CUD. Realisations closer than that of RP (in terms of tongue-height) were marked *RP+*; those that were more open than that of CUD were marked *CUD+*; and those that fell between the RP and CUD realisations were called *blends* (for want of a better term). The diagram below illustrates the principle:

$$- - - [e] - - - - [ȩ] - - - - [ɛ] - - - - [ɛ] - - - - [ɛ] - - -$$
$$\quad RP+ \qquad RP \qquad blend \qquad CUD \qquad CUD+$$

A similar method was used with other features.

In the case of the differences of incidence and the phonemic differences (features 1–6), blends were held to occur in cases of inconsistency. For example, an informant might use /AR/ in *laugh* but /A/ in *glass*; this would be taken to be a basic CUD pronunciation, modified under the influence of RP, and classed as a blend.

The terms RP+ and CUD+ should be taken merely as convenient labels. It is true that some features marked RP+ happen to reflect recent tendencies in RP (e.g. closer realisations of /E/ and /A/) and it is possible that some CUD+ features represent a more archaic state of the local accent; but on the whole it would be misleading to equate RP+ everywhere with 'advanced RP' or CUD+ with 'archaic CUD'.

This process of assignment was carried out for each of the twenty-three features of the speech of each informant; each feature was marked as either (i) RP+, or (ii) RP, or (iii) blend, or (iv) CUD, or (v) CUD+, or (vi) may not have been assignable to one of the other five classes. (The assignments are shown in Tables 27 and 28 of Appendix II; Table 29 gives the number of features in each class.) Very few features are unassignable; most informants have no such features, a few have one or two. The exceptions are four informants with a majority of unassignable features; and these turn out to be the two Scots and the two people from Tyneside referred to in Chapter II, page 22.

It is now possible to provide a linguistic classification of all eighty informants. This is done by putting them into two lists, given in Table 17 below. The left-hand column shows the number of features of pronunciation which are the same as in CUD; these are given in descending order. The right-hand column shows the number of features that are the same as in RP; these are given in ascending order. CUD and CUD+ features have been lumped together, as have RP and RP+ features; the CUD+ and RP+ figures are given in brackets next to the total. In both lists the maximum possible figure is 23, the number of features studied.

TABLE 17

Informant No.	CUD/CUD+	Informant No.	RP/RP+
93	21(7)	73	0
89	21(5)	93	1(0)
48	20(7)	92	1(0)
85	20(5)	87	1(0)
4	20(5)	78	1(1)
78	20(4)	9	1(1)
71	20(4)	4	2(0)
84	20(3)	85	2(0)
92	20(1)	71	2(0)
22	19(6)	88	2(0)
13	19(4) ·	89	2(1)
88	19(3)	48	2(1)
30	19(3)	22	2(1)
19	18(5)	84	3(0)
20	18(4)	30	3(0)
5	18(4)	20	3(0)
80	18(3)	64	3(0)
9	18(3)	45	3(0)
87	17(5)	49	3(0)
64	17(4)	39	3(0)
45	17(3)	44	3(0)
40	17(2)	13	3(1)
73	17(0)	80	3(1)
36	16(4)	40	4(0)
69	16(4)	69	4(0)
33	16(4)	36	4(0)
10	16(4)	12	4(0)
49	16(3)	53	4(0)
43	16(3)	19	4(1)
74	16(3)	5	4(1)
39	16(2)	33	5(0)
55	15(4)	43	5(0)
14	15(4)	45	5(0)
42	15(4)	37	5(0)
23	15(3)	75	5(0)

TABLE 17 (cont.)

Informant No.	CUD/CUD+	Informant No.	RP/RP+
37	15(2)	10	5(1)
66	15(2)	86	5(1)
54	14(4)	14	5(2)
15	14(2)	56	5(2)
56	14(2)	26	6(0)
8	14(2)	74	6(1)
21	14(2)	8	6(1)
44	14(1)	21	6(1)
83	13(5)	34	6(1)
52	13(4)	41	6(1)
1	13(3)	42	6(2)
35	13(3)	66	6(2)
63	13(3)	54	6(2)
91	13(2)	1	7(0)
26	12(5)	23	7(1)
34	12(5)	50	7(1)
86	12(4)	35	7(2)
62	12(3)	76	7(2)
18	12(2)	62	8(0)
76	11(4)	15	8(1)
67	11(3)	63	8(1)
41	11(2)	91	8(1)
7	11(2)	7	8(1)
50	10(4)	83	8(2)
72	9(1)	31	8(2)
25	8(0)	67	8(4)
12	6(2)	18	9(1)
61	6(2)	52	10(0)
38	6(1)	25	11(1)
77	5(3)	77	11(2)
31	5(1)	61	12(1)
3	5(1)	3	12(1)
68	5(1)	72	12(3)
11	5(0)	11	13(1)
57	5(0)	60	14(2)
51	5(0)	57	14(3)
65	4(3)	38	15(1)
16	4(2)	29	16(1)
53	4(1)	46	16(1)
29	4(1)	51	16(2)
60	4(0)	65	16(3)
46	4(0)	28	17(3)
28	3(2)	68	17(5)
75	3(1)	16	18(1)
82	3(0)	82	18(2)

Where a group of informants had the same figure in either column, their figure in the other column is used for ranking purposes.

In each of these lists lines have been drawn across at sixteen or more features (representing a 2/3 majority) and at twelve to fifteen features (representing a 50% majority). It happens that these divisions are mutually exclusive, since no informant with twelve or more RP features (for instance) can have more than eleven CUD features, as the total possible is twenty-three. We use these divisions to set up six linguistic classes of informants, defined in the following section.

The linguistic classification

Class A contains those informants with sixteen or more features assignable as either CUD or CUD+. There are 31 such informants, 38¾% of the total. In descending order they are Informants Nos. 93, 89, 48, 85, 4, 78, 71, 84, 92, 22, 13, 88, 30, 19, 20, 5, 80, 9, 87, 64, 45, 40, 73, 36, 69, 33, 10, 49, 43, 74, 39.

Class B contains those informants with twelve to fifteen CUD or CUD+ features: 23 informants, 28¾% of the total. In descending order they are Informants Nos. 55, 14, 42, 23, 37, 66, 54, 15, 56, 8, 21, 44, 83, 52, 1, 35, 63, 91, 26, 34, 86, 62, 18.

Class C contains, with a few exceptions, those informants with eleven or fewer RP features *and* eleven or fewer CUD features: 7 informants, 8¾% of the total. They are Informants Nos. 7, 25, 41, 50, 67, 76, 77.

Class D contains those informants with twelve to fifteen RP or RP+ features: 7 informants, 8¾% of the total. In descending order they are Informants Nos. 38, 57, 60, 11, 72, 3, 61.

Class E contains those informants with sixteen or more RP or RP+ features: 8 informants, 10% of the total. In descending order they are Informants Nos. 82, 16, 68, 28, 65, 51, 46, 29.

Class F contains those informants with a majority of features unassignable to either CUD or RP: 4 informants, 5% of the total. They stand out in Table 28 of Appendix II: Informant No. 12 is a 'Geordie' with thirteen unassignable features; No. 31, with eight such features is also a Northumbrian; No. 53, with thirteen unassignable features, is a Scot; as is No. 75, with fourteen such features. These four informants are the only ones who appear in widely separated positions in the two lists of Table 17 above. Since their speech is largely not describable in terms of the parameters set up for this study, no further linguistic work will be done on Class F.

The reader should note the large number of informants who fall into Classes A and B, those with a majority of CUD features: 54 informants, $67\frac{1}{2}\%$ of the total.

We now want a description of the speech of the average member of each linguistic class. In order to set up the classification it was only necessary to know how many features of pronunciation were to be categorised as RP, CUD or blend; for a full description of the classes we must show exactly which features are involved.

The assignments of features given in Appendix II are repeated in a more easily digestible form in Appendix III. The operation has been simplified by drawing no distinction between CUD and CUD+, or between RP and RP+. The final table of Appendix III (page 124) gathers this information together and categorises the features of pronunciation of the average member of each class.

A re-ordered version of this summary table is presented in Table 18 opposite. The principle of the re-ordering is that features with CUD or CUD+ realisations in all five classes appear at the top of the table, while features with such realisations in Class A only are placed at the bottom. The meaning of the symbols is as follows:

C indicates a majority of CUD or CUD+ features;
R indicates a majority of RP or RP+ features;
B indicates a majority of blends;
I indicates a majority of unassignable features.

Symbols in brackets mean that the majority is less than 50%; two symbols separated by an oblique stroke imply an equal number of features.

As the reader casts his eye across Table 18 from Class A to Class E, most features show a smooth transition from C-forms to R-forms, sometimes via blends. For three features (2, 10 and 13) the transition is not smooth, and they have had to be placed on the table in a somewhat arbitrary manner; their feature numbers are bracketed. The five features which include blends (1, 4, 11, 12 and 17) are also difficult to place; the criterion used is whether the blends resemble the C-forms or the R-forms the more closely. So for features 1 and 11, B has been taken to be equivalent to R, whereas for features 4, 12 and 17 it has been taken to be equivalent to C.

The dotted lines drawn across the table divide the features into five groups according to how far towards Class E the C-forms spread. Within each group no reliance should be placed upon the order of features.

TABLE 18
(Compare Table 31, page 124)

Feature		Class A	Class B	Class C	Class D	Class E
3	/NG/	C	C	C	C	C
7	/Ā/	C	C	C	(C)	R
14	/A/	C	C	C	C	R
1	*laugh*, etc.	C	C	C	B	R
5	vowel + /R/	C	C/R	C	R	R
19	/O/	C	C	C	(R)	R
20	/AR/	C	C	C	R	R
22	/OR/	C	C	C	R	R
18	/Q/	C	C	C	(C/R)	R
12	/Õ/	C	(B)	(B)	(R)	R
11	/Q̄/	C	C	C	B	B
(10)	/Ou/	C	C	C	R	C
17	/U/	C/B	B	B	(B/R)	R
(13)	/Oi/	(R)	(C)	(I)	R	R
(2)	*one*	C	C	R	C	R
8	/Ē/	C	C	R	R	R
15	/E/	C	(C)	R	(B/R)	R
21	/ER/	C	C	(R)	R	R
16	/I/	C	C	R	R	R
9	/Ĭ/	C	R	(R)	R	R
6	/H/	C	R	R	R	R
23	/ĀR/	C	R	R	R	R
4	/U/–/Q/	B	R	R	R	R

Anticipating for a moment one of the results of the survey, we can say that in Cannock, as in many other English urban areas, greater education and higher social class correlate with increasing influence of RP. The object of producing the re-ordered Table 18 was to see which features of pronunciation are the first to be affected by RP influences, and which are the most resistant. The first rough draft of the table was drawn up using only feature numbers, with no expectation that the groupings would prove to be significant; but when the feature labels were added, two interesting and quite unexpected results emerged at once.

(1) The increasing effect of RP influence can be seen by reading Table 18 from the bottom upwards. The interesting aspect of this is that there are phonetic similarities between the groups of features that are affected together. The salient points are as follows:

The CUD accent, as defined in Chapter IV, has no contrast between /U/ and /Q/: *bud, bull, dull, rubber, put, pudding, butter* all have the vowel /Q/. Even in Class A, however, only a minority of informants lack this contrast in their speech: most have the contrast but use it inconsistently, e.g. Informant No. 39 uses /U/ in *bud, dull, butter* but has /Q/ in *rubber*. Where /U/ occurs, its realisation is usually [ʌ], a more retracted sound than RP [ɐ]. Moving on to Class B, we find the RP distribution of /Q/ and /U/ established consistently, though not the RP pronunciation of /U/.

The other far-reaching effect of RP influence is the acquisition of /H/. Very few Class A informants are without /H/ altogether, though most of them use it only sporadically. In Class B it is established as a normal phoneme.

Continuing to read Table 18 upwards, we find that the *front vowels and diphthongs* retain CUD realisations into Class B, but yield to RP influence in Class C; whereas the *back vowels and diphthongs* are more resistant, with CUD forms being normal in Class C. At the top of the table, the clearly-pronounced /G/ of *sing, singer* and *singing* is still to be heard among the majority of Class E informants.

(2) Even more interesting is the fact that the base vowel phonemes succumb to RP influence at the same time as their corresponding 'short' variants. So /Ā/ and /A/ survive in CUD form as far as Class D; /Ē/ and /E/ to Class B; /Ō/ and /O/, /Q̄/ and /Q/, /Ou/ and /U/ all retain CUD realisations into Class C. /Ī/ and /I/ appear in adjacent groups.

In Modern English, whether CUD or RP, there is no longer any phonetic connection between the base vowel phonemes and their 'short' variants. But in Middle English, prior to the operation of the Great Vowel Shift (which began in the fifteenth century), there was a simple phonetic relationship between them, namely length.

The following diagram shows the vowel system of Middle English:

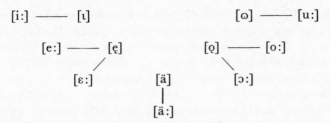

In general, the effect of the Great Vowel Shift was to change the long vowels into the modern diphthongs. In the course of this process [e:] and [ɛ:] have coalesced in both RP and CUD (so that *meat* and *meet* are now homophones), whereas [o:] and [ɔ:] have remained distinct. In addition, in RP only, the short high back vowel [ʊ] has split into [ʊ] and [ɐ].

The reflexes of the Middle English vowels in RP are as follows:

$$
\begin{array}{ccc}
& & [ɐ] \\
& & \diagdown \\
[äɪ] \text{—} [ɪ] & [ʊ] \text{—} [äʊ] \\[2mm]
[ʉi] \text{—} [ɛ] & [ɒ] \text{—} [ʊu] \\
& & \diagdown \\
[æ] & [əʊ] \\
| \\
[ɛɪ]
\end{array}
$$

And in CUD:

$$
\begin{array}{ccc}
[äɪ] \text{—} [ɪ] & [ʊ] \text{—} [äʊ] \\[2mm]
[ʉi] \text{—} [ɛ] & [ɒ] \text{—} [ʔü] \\
& & \diagdown \\
[a] & [ʔʊ] \\
| \\
[ɛɪ]
\end{array}
$$

In strictly phonetic terms, the Middle English links between the base vowel phonemes and their 'short' variants have been broken in modern English; but as was pointed out at the beginning of

Chapter IV (pages 39 and 40), the connections can still be seen in morpho-phonemic and morphological alternations. The fact that in Cannock these pairs of short vowel and corresponding diphthong are influenced together by the prestige dialect might indicate that some affinity between them is still unconsciously felt.

The present writer has no theory to explain why, in Cannock, front vowels should be more susceptible to RP influence than back vowels. Certainly the effect is very marked, and if one looks through Appendix II, Table 28, it will be noticed that there are a number of informants who have, for example, an RP realisation of /Ē/ but a CUD realisation of /Q̄/.

We conclude this chapter with a description of the average member of each of the five linguistic classes of informants.

Class A

Class A comprises those informants with at least a two-thirds majority of CUD or CUD+ features. By definition, at least sixteen of the twenty-three features will be of this type; in fact Table 18 shows that the class as a whole has twenty CUD or CUD+ features.

1. *Laugh, dance* and *glass* all have the vowel /A/. CUD.
2. *One* has the vowel /O/. CUD.
3. The /G/ is pronounced in *sing, singer* and *singing*. CUD.
4. The contrast between /U/ and /Q/ usually occurred in some words but not in others (e.g. *bud* might be [b̥ɒd̥] but *butter* [b̥ʌ̈tə]), or sometimes there might be cases of hypercorrection (e.g. very commonly *put* = [p'ʌ̈t]). blend.
5. Realisations of the sequence 'base vowel + /R/' are disyllabic, the /R/ having the value [ə]. CUD.
6. /H/ is either missing altogether or occurs only rarely. CUD.

7. /Ã/ = [ɛɩ] CUD.	16. /I/ = [ɩ̈] CUD.
8. /Ē/ = [ɩ̈i] CUD.	17. /U/ (see below)
9. /Ī/ = [ä̈ɩ] CUD.	18. /Q/ = [ɷ] CUD.
10. /Ou/ = [ä̈ɷ] CUD.	19. /O/ = [ɒ] CUD.
11. /Q̄/ = [ə̈ü] CUD.	20. /AR/ = [ä̈:] CUD.
12. /Ō/ = [ɔɷ] CUD.	21. /ER/ = [ə̈:] CUD.
13. /Oi/ = [ɔɩ] RP.	22. /OR/ = [ɔ̈:] CUD.
14. /A/ = [a] CUD.	23. /ÃR/ = [ɛ:] CUD.
15. /E/ = [ɛ] CUD.	

Note on no. 17, i.e. the realisation of /U/. This feature is obviously closely connected with no. 4. Here, CUD features and blends occur in roughly equal numbers. Classification as CUD means that /U/ does not occur; a blend means that /U/ is present but with a non-RP realisation.

Class B

Class B comprises those informants having a half to two-thirds majority of CUD or CUD+ features. This means the number of such features must be between twelve and fifteen; the average for the class is in fact fifteen, compared with twenty for Class A. With one exception, the CUD features of Class B are also CUD in Class A, as one would expect; the exception is no. 13 /Oi/, which had an RP majority in Class A.

In Class B there are five features which were CUD in Class A, but not here: nos. 5, 6, 9, 12 and 23.

1. *Laugh, dance* and *glass* all have the vowel /A/. CUD.
2. *One* has the vowel /O/. CUD.
3. The /G/ is pronounced in *sing, singer* and *singing*. CUD.
4. The contrast between /U/ and /Q/ is present and used correctly. RP.
5. Monophonemic and disyllabic realisations of ' base vowel + /R/ ' occur in approximately equal proportions.

6. /H/ is used correctly. RP.
7. /Ā/ = [εɩ] CUD.
8. /Ē/ = [ÿi] CUD.
9. /Ī/ = [äɩ] RP.
10. /Ou/ = [äɷ] CUD.
11. /Q̄/ = [əü] CUD.
12. /Ō/ = [ɔ̈ɷ] blend.
13. /Oi/ = [ɔɩ] CUD.
14. /A/ = [a] CUD.

15. /E/ = [ε] CUD.
16. /I/ = [ɪ] CUD.
17. /U/ = [ʌ] blend.
18. /Q/ = [ɷ] CUD.
19. /O/ = [ɒ] CUD.
20. /AR/ = [ä:] CUD.
21. /ER/ = [ə:] CUD.
22. /OR/ = [ɔ:] CUD.
23. /ĀR/ = [εə] RP.

Class C

Class C comprises those informants whose speech has less than twelve CUD features *and* less than twelve RP features. On the average, in fact, the balance is still towards CUD, with eleven CUD features, nine RP and two blends. All the CUD features of Class C were also CUD in Classes A and B; the two blends were blends in Class B;

and there are five features which were CUD in Classes A and B, but not in Class C: nos. 2, 8, 15, 16 and 21.

1. *Laugh, dance* and *glass* all have the vowel /A/. CUD.
2. *One* has the vowel /U/. RP.
3. The /G/ is pronounced in *sing, singer* and *singing*. CUD.
4. The contrast between /U/ and /Q/ is present and used correctly. RP.
5. Realisations of the sequence 'base vowel + /R/' are disyllabic, the /R/ having the value [ə]. CUD.

6. /H/ is used correctly. RP.	15. /E/ = [ɛ̝] RP.
7. /Ā/ = [ɛɪ] CUD.	16. /I/ = [ɪ] RP.
8. /Ē/ = [ʉi] RP.	17. /U/ = [ʌ̈] blend.
9. /Ī/ = [äɪ] RP.	18. /Q/ = [ɑ] CUD.
10. /Ou/ = [äʊ] CUD.	19. /O/ = [ɒ] CUD.
11. /Q̄/ = [əü] CUD.	20. /AR/ = [ä:] CUD.
12. /Ō/ = [ɔʊ] blend.	21. /ER/ = [ə:] RP.
13. /Oi/ (see below)	22. /OR/ = [ɔ:] CUD.
14. /A/ = [a] CUD.	23. /ĀR/ = [ɛə] RP.

Note on no. 13: In Class C a majority of the realisations of this feature are not readily assignable to either RP or CUD.

Class D

Class D comprises those informants having a half to two-thirds majority of RP features. This means that the number of RP features must be between twelve and fifteen; the average for the class is fourteen RP features, compared with twenty for Class E. With one exception, the RP features of Class D are also RP in Class E, as is to be expected; the exception is no. 10 /Ou/, which has a CUD majority in Class E.

In Class D there are seven features which are clearly RP in Class E, but not in Class D: nos. 1, 2, 7, 14, 15, 17 and 18.

1. *Laugh, dance, glass:* a small majority of Class D informants are inconsistent, using /A/ in some words and /AR/ in others. blend.
2. *One* has the vowel /O/. CUD.
3. The /G/ is pronounced in *sing, singer* and *singing*. CUD.
4. The contrast between /U/ and /Q/ is present and used correctly. RP.
5. Realisations of the sequence 'base vowel + /R/' are mono-phonemic. RP.

6. /H/ is used correctly. RP.
7. /Ā/ = [ɛɪ] CUD.
8. /Ē/ = [ɪi] RP.
9. /Ī/ = [äɪ] RP.
10. /Ou/ = [äɷ] RP.
11. /Q̄/ = [əu]/[ʉu] blend.
12. /O/ = [əɷ] RP.
13. /Oi/ = [ɔɪ] RP.
14. /A/ = [a] CUD.

15. /E/ = [ɛ] RP.
16. /I/ = [ɪ] RP.
17. /U/ = [ʌ̈] blend.
18. /Q/ = [ɷ] blend.
19. /O/ = [ɒ] RP.
20. /AR/ = [ä:] RP.
21. /ER/ = [ə:] RP.
22. /OR/ = [ɔ:] RP.
23. /ĀR/ = [ɛə] RP.

Class E

Class E comprises those informants whose speech has at least a two-thirds majority of RP features. By definition, at least sixteen of the twenty-three features will be classed as RP; in fact the class as a whole has twenty RP features.

1. *Laugh, dance* and *glass* all have the vowel /AR/. RP.
2. *One* has the vowel /U/. RP.
3. The /G/ is pronounced in *sing, singer* and *singing.* CUD.
4. The contrast between /U/ and /Q/ is present and used correctly. RP.
5. Realisations of the sequence 'base vowel + /R/' are monophonemic. RP.
6. /H/ is used correctly. RP.
7. /Ā/ = [ɛɪ] RP.
8. /Ē/ = [ɪi] RP.
9. /Ī/ = [äɪ] RP.
10. /Ou/ = [äɷ] CUD.
11. /Q̄/ = [əu]/[ʉu] blend.
12. /Ō/ = [əɷ] RP.
13. /Oi/ = [ɔɪ] RP.
14. /A/ = [æ] RP.

15. /E/ = [ɛ] RP.
16. /I/ = [ɪ] RP.
17. /U/ = [ɐ] RP.
18. /Q/ = [ɷ] RP.
19. /O/ = [ɒ] RP.
20. /AR/ = [ä:] RP.
21. /ER/ = [ə:] RP.
22. /OR/ = [ɔ:] RP.
23. /ĀR/ = [ɛə] RP.

CHAPTER VI

The statistical analysis

We have now carried out two classifications of the eighty informants. In Chapter II they were classified according to various features of their social, geographic and economic background; and in Chapter V they were classified again, this time by purely linguistic criteria. The next stage of the research is to compare these independently obtained sets of results. From this procedure we hope to be able to answer the question: is there any significant relationsip between a background classification and the five linguistic classes set up in the previous chapter?

The process of comparison has two stages: first, the subjection of each set of figures to the statistical test called χ^2, and secondly, the interpretation of the results so obtained. It is vital that the two stages should not be confused: one can 'prove' anything by a false interpretation of statistical tests.

χ^2 test

To illustrate the method we will use the χ^2 test to see if there is any significant correlation between the *sex* of informants and their *linguistic* classification.

First we tabulate the *observed data* in chart form, as follows:

TABLE 19

	Class A	Class B	Classes C, D and E	
Male	27	7	7	(41)
Female	4	16	15	(35)
	(31)	(23)	(22)	(76)

The figures in each *cell* of the chart are numbers of informants, those in brackets are the sums of the rows and columns. The bracketed figure in the bottom right-hand corner is the grand total, equal to the number of informants involved. This figure, seventy-six, is four less than the number of informants interviewed, because members of Linguistic Class F (all men) have been excluded (see above, p. 59).

The χ^2 test becomes unreliable if very small figures appear in a cell. For this reason only a very broad background classification was used in Chapter II, and in all the statistical tests it has been necessary to combine Linguistic Classes C, D and E.

We now make the *null hypothesis* that there is *no* correlation between the two sets of observed data; the χ^2 test will tell us whether the null hypothesis is likely to be true or not. It is necessary to calculate what the figures in each cell of the chart would be if the null hypothesis were true; these figures are called the *expected data*. The bracketed row and column totals must be the same as for the observed data, so the expected figure for a cell is obtained by multiplying together the totals of the row and column in which it appears, and then dividing the product by the grand total, seventy-six. E.g. the expected figure for Class A Males is $(41 \times 31) \div 76 = 16 \cdot 8$.

These results are tabulated in a similar way to produce a chart of *expected data*, as follows:

TABLE 20

	Class A	Class B	Classes C, D and E	
Males	16·8	12·4	11·8	(41)
Females	14·2	10·6	10·2	(35)
	(31)	(23)	(22)	(76)

A moment's thought will show that it is not necessary to calculate the expected figure for every cell: since the row and column totals are known, some figures can be ascertained by simple subtraction. In a '3 × 2' chart like this one, two cell-values must be calculated by multiplication and division; there are said to be two *degrees of freedom*. A '3 × 3' will have four degrees of freedom, and a '2 × 2' chart only one—but with one degree of freedom the χ^2 test is unreliable and should not be applied.

Calling the observed data O and the expected data E, the value of χ^2 can now be calculated, using the formula:

$$\chi^2 = \sum \frac{(O-E)^2}{E}$$

that is to say, the value of $\dfrac{(O-E)^2}{E}$ is calculated for each cell, and the results for all the cells are added together.

Published tables of χ^2 show, for different degrees of freedom, what value χ^2 must attain or exceed before one can regard the null hypothesis as disproved, at various levels of certainty. A relevant extract is given here:

TABLE 21
(Value of χ^2)

Degree of freedom	Percentage level					
	10%	5%	2·5%	1%	0·5%	0·1%
2	4·61	5·99	7·38	9·21	10·60	13·81
4	7·78	9·49	11·14	13·28	14·86	18·47

When χ^2 is calculated using the data of Tables 19 and 20, the value comes to 22·85. There are two degrees of freedom in this case, and the value of χ^2 is well in excess of the 13·81 required for certainty at the 0·1% level. This means that there is less than one chance in a thousand that the observed data would be produced if the null hypothesis were true; we may therefore safely regard it as false, and conclude that there *is* a significant correlation between the figures for sex and linguistic class. And that is all we may conclude at this stage; we have not yet interpreted the result, and we cannot yet say that any causal relationship is proved between the items being tested.

Appendix IV gives the results of applying the χ^2 test to the survey material. There the fivefold linguistic classification has been compared separately with background classification by sex, age, income group, social class, place of birth, length of time lived in Cannock Urban District, and length of schooling. Following this, the various types of background classifications have been compared among themselves. This may seem wasteful, but it has been done in order that no significant relationship might be overlooked. Even so, three combinations could not be tested: (a) sex and income group, (b) sex and length of schooling, and (c) income group and length of schooling. The figures for each of these combinations would produce '2×2' charts with one degree of freedom, to which the χ^2 test is not applicable.

For each test of significance that we perform, we compare the calculated value of χ^2 with the figures given in Table 21 above, and draw conclusions as follows:

(i) If the value of χ^2 exceeds that given under 0·1%, we conclude that it is at least 99·9% certain that there is a significant relationship between the classes in question;

(ii) if it exceeds that given under 0·5%, it is at least 99·5% certain that there is a relationship;

(iii) if it exceeds that given under 1%, it is at least 99% certain that there is a relationship;

(iv) if it exceeds that given under 2·5%, it is at least 97·5% certain that there is a relationship;

(v) if it exceeds that given under 5%, it is at least 95% certain that there is a relationship;

(vi) if it exceeds that given under 10% it is at least 90% certain that there is a relationship;

(vii) if it does not reach that given under 10%, it is less than 90% certain that there is a relationship; but this is not good enough, and we take this to mean there is *no* relationship.

There is a possible cause of misunderstanding here. The χ^2 test does *not* show how strong the relationship is between sets of figures; it merely shows how certain one can be that such a relationship actually exists.

The results of the statistical tests in Appendix IV are summarised in Table 22 below. In each square it is indicated whether a relationship exists between the parameters that intersect there: a figure shows at what percentage level the relationship is significant, and X means that there is no significant relationship, i.e. the value of χ^2 did not reach the 10% level. The three combinations to which the test could not be applied have been left blank.

The results of the χ^2 tests will be interpreted in the following chapter. The reader should remember, however, that a high value of χ^2 does not, in itself, prove anything; the data must be carefully scrutinised before any conclusions about cause-and-effect relationships may be drawn. A frivolous example may serve as a warning: there is a high correlation between the number of radio licences issued between 1930 and 1950, and the number of people certified insane during the same period. We would be foolish to conclude, on that 'evidence', that listening to the radio causes madness!

TABLE 22

(χ^2 test results)

	Linguistic class	Sex	Age	Income group	Social class	Place of birth	Time lived in Cannock	Length of schooling
Linguistic class								
Sex	0·1							
Age	2·5	X						
Income group	2·5		0·1					
Social class	0·1	5·0	2·5	5·0				
Place of birth	1·0	X	X	X	2·5			
Time lived in Cannock	X	X	5·0	X	5·0	0·5		
Length of schooling	0·5		X		0·1	0·5	5·0	

CHAPTER VII

The results of the survey

The results of applying the χ^2 significance test to the survey material have been summarised in Table 22 on page 72. There we find significantly high values of χ^2 in seventeen cases. But this was a mechanical process; it is also necessary to study the results carefully to see what interpretation can be put on them.

It soon becomes apparent that not all of the seventeen correlations are of equal value. Seven of them in fact, cannot be used, for the following reasons:

There are two cases where the sets of figures under comparison are not entirely independent of each other and where a meaningless correlation is thus produced. They are *Age and Income Group*—income necessarily declines with age since most people in the 'elderly' class are pensioners; and *Place of Birth and Time lived in Cannock*—because the longer one has lived in a place, the more likely it is that one was born there. It would be unwise to build any theories on these two 'results'.

Where the χ^2 test gives a result that is significant at the 0·1%, 0·5% or 1% levels, we can safely consider a connection to be proved between the sets of data concerned. At the 2·5% or 5% levels, however, we must be more cautious: the possibility that the observed data may be produced fortuitously is strong enough to be taken into account. In such cases we must look at the data itself, to see where the observed figures are higher than the expected ones. If these 'higher-than-expected' figures form a clear line across the chart, e.g.

$$\begin{array}{ccc} + & 0 & 0 \\ 0 & + & 0 \\ 0 & 0 & + \end{array} \qquad \text{or} \qquad \begin{array}{ccc} 0 & + & + \\ + & 0 & 0 \\ 0 & 0 & 0, \end{array}$$

then we can safely assume that there is a significant relationship between the two sets of figures. But if the 'higher-than-expected' figures form a haphazard pattern such as these:

$$
\begin{array}{cccccccc}
+ & 0 & + & & & 0 & 0 & + \\
+ & + & 0 & & \text{or} & + & 0 & 0 \\
0 & 0 & 0 & & & 0 & + & 0
\end{array}
$$

then what conclusions can one possibly draw?

Four of the χ^2 tests yielded results significant only at the 2·5% level, and five at the 5% level. A study of the patterns formed by the figures showed that in four cases there was a line across the chart, but that in five other cases there was no clear pattern. These five correlations are therefore not used in interpreting the results: they are *Linguistic Class with Age, Age with Social Class, Social Class with Place of Birth, Age with Time lived in Cannock* and *Social Class with Time lived in Cannock*.

Having completed this process of elimination, we are left with ten significant realtionships for further consideration:

At the 0·1% level:

(a) Linguistic Class with Sex;

(b) Linguistic Class with Social Class;

(c) Social Class with Length of Schooling;

At the 0·5% level:

(d) Linguistic Class with Length of Schooling;

(e) Place of Birth with Length of Schooling;

At the 1% level:

(f) Linguistic Class with Place of Birth;

At the 2·5% level:

(g) Linguistic Class with Income Group;

At the 5% level:

(h) Sex with Social Class;

(i) Income Group with Social Class;

(j) Time lived in Cannock with Length of Schooling.

Comparing this list with Table 22, we notice that all the parameters listed there appear in the above list, *except Age*. Of the χ^2 tests involving age, only four gave a positive result; of these, three have been eliminated because there is no clear pattern in the charts, and the other one (*Age and Income Group*) because there is an inbuilt relationship between the two sets of data. This means that whatever conclusions we may come to about factors determining linguistic classification, Age will not be one of them, even as an indirect influence.

This result, though negative, is nevertheless important, since it indicates that, whatever else the 'Cannock accent' (part of Class A) may be, it is not a way of speech characteristic of the elderly, as one might have expected, or indeed of any other age-group. There is therefore no evidence that the 'Cannock accent', as defined in Chapter IV, is dying out. Not that this is entirely unexpected—it is, after all, easy to hear the 'broadest' of accents from children playing in the street.

The ten significant correlations

(a) *Linguistic Class with Sex:* men predominate in Linguistic Class A, and women in Classes B, C, D and E.

(b) *Linguistic Class with Social Class:* Skilled Manual and Semi-skilled workers predominate in Linguistic Classes A and B, whereas Intermediate and Skilled Non-manual workers predominate in Classes C, D and E.

(c) *Social Class with Length of Schooling:* most Intermediate and Skilled Non-manual workers had stayed on at school beyond the minimum leaving age at the time, whereas most Skilled Manual and Semi-skilled workers had left school as soon as possible.

(d) *Linguistic Class with Length of Schooling:* all Class A speakers had left school as soon as possible, but people with extra schooling predominate in Classes B, C, D and E.

(e) *Place of Birth with Length of Schooling:* among those born in Cannock, there is a preponderance of people with minimum education, whereas people born outside the Urban District are more likely to have stayed on at school.

(f) *Linguistic Class with Place of Birth:* Class A speakers were mostly born in Cannock, Class B speakers up to fourteen miles away (i.e. in other parts of South Staffordshire), whereas people in Classes C, D and E were for the most part born outside the county.

(g) *Linguistic Class with Income Group:* people earning less than £1,000 predominate in Linguistic Classes A and B, and those earning more than that figure in Classes C, D and E.

(h) *Sex with Social Class:* there is a majority of women among Intermediate and Skilled Non-manual workers, and of men among Skilled Manual and Semi-skilled workers.

(i) *Income Group with Social Class:* there is a preponderance of people earning more than £1,000 among Intermediate and Skilled Non-manual workers, and of people earning less than £1,000 among Skilled Manual and Semi-skilled workers.

(j) *Time lived in Cannock with Length of Schooling:* People who have lived their whole life in Cannock are more likely to have left school at the minimum age; whereas those who have lived less than half their life in Cannock are likely to have stayed on at school.

Five of these results compare Linguistic Class with one of the background parameters (a, b, d, f and g). Four of these confirm what we would have expected from casual observation: it is not surprising that members of the higher social classes are more subject to RP influence, nor that such influence is also connected with higher income and extended education—and these three factors are obviously interrelated. It is also predictable that the 'Cannock accent' should be less in evidence among those who were not born there—it remains to be considered whether there is any connection between this fact and the social influences. What one would probably not have predicted is result (a): it appears that the speech of men is 'broader' than that of women.

Remembering that the reason for testing the background parameters among themselves was to avoid the risk of overlooking some unexpected correlation, we now consider the five such tests that turn out to be significant (c, e, h, i and j). We are not surprised to find a relationship between Social Class and extent of education, or between Social Class and Income Group—though if the latter test were to be repeated today, twelve years after the survey, the dividing line would be well above £1,000! Nor is it entirely unexpected that Social Class is linked with Sex—after all, most manual workers are men. But the connection between Length of Schooling and Place of Birth and Time lived in Cannock was not, one may think, predictable. Even so, faced with these results, it is not difficult to work out why they should be: people who have benefited from extra schooling are likely to have entered occupations which have taken them out of the area of their birth. Results (e) and (j) do, in fact, reflect the greater mobility of the better-educated higher social classes.

The interrelationships between the categories involved in these ten correlations are summarised in the following diagram. (It has already been shown, page 73, that Place of Birth and Time lived in Cannock are automatically connected.)

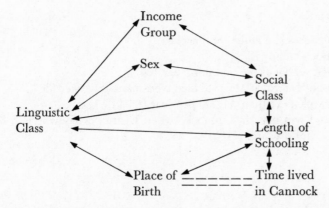

When one is doing statistical work with classes and figures, it is very easy to forget that real people form the basis of it all. As a partial correction to this tendency, there now follows a brief description of the average member of each linguistic class. (This has already been done, from the phonological point of view, at the end of Chapter V, pages 64 to 67.) After each statement, the percentage of class-members who conform to the average is given. Age is not mentioned, since we have shown that it appears to have no linguistic significance.

Class A

The average member of this class
  is a man (87%),
  left school at the minimum age (all),
  is a Skilled Manual or Semi-skilled worker (97%),
  earns less than £1,000 per year (61%),
  and was born in Cannock Urban District or elsewhere in South
    Staffordshire (97%).

Class B

The average member of this class
  is a woman (70%),
  left school at the minimum age (78%),
  is a Skilled Manual or Semi-skilled worker (70%),
  earns less than £1,000 per year (65%),
  and was born in Cannock Urban District or elsewhere in South
    Staffordshire (90%).

Class C

The average member of this class
   is a woman (72%),
   left school at the minimum age (86%),
   is an Intermediate or Skilled Non-manual worker (86%),
   earns more than £1,000 per year (86%),
   and was born in Cannock Urban District or elsewhere in South
      Staffordshire (71%).

Class D

The average member of this class
   is a woman (86%),
   left school at the minimum age (72%),
   is an Intermediate or Skilled Non-manual worker (72%),
   earns more than £1,000 per year (72%),
   and was born in Cannock Urban District or elsewhere in South
      Staffordshire (57%).

Class E

The average member of this class
   stayed on at school for at least one extra year (62%),
   is an Intermediate or Skilled Non-manual worker (75%),
   earns more than £1,000 per year (75%),
   and was born in Cannock Urban District or elsewhere in South
      Staffordshire (62%).
   (There is an equal number of men and women in this class.)

If we study the above descriptions, and reflect upon the correlations we have established between the background parameters, we
can not only gain an impression of what sort of person the average
member of each linguistic class is, but also begin to see what factors
are the most influencial in determining classification. There were
three correlations between pairs of background parameters which
we were not surprised to find: Social Class with Income Group,

Social Class with Sex, and Social Class with Length of Schooling. We will consider each of these in turn.

Social Class and Income Group. In the description of average members of the linguistic classes, we can establish a dividing line between Classes B and C in respect of Social Class, and also in respect of Income Group. On one side of the line, in Classes C, D and E, these two categories fuse: all Intermediate and Skilled Non-manual workers earn more than £1,000 per year. On the other side, the two categories are almost united in Class B, but in Class A only two-thirds of the Skilled Manual and semi-skilled workers earn less than £1,000 per year. A little thought suggests that, in all probability, the Income Group is only significant as a partial reflection of Social Class; since although salaries are usually fairly high, wages are not necessarily low, especially when overtime payments are considered. We conclude that Social Class is the important factor here, and that the connection between Linguistic Class and Income Group is a reflection of the relationship of both these categories to Social Class.

Social Class and Sex. Here the clearest dividing line is between Classes A and B, which in other respects are virtually the same. It almost seems as if the male Skilled Manual or Semi-skilled worker is a Class A speaker, while his wife occupies Class B! The men of Class A are occupied in heavy work: they are welders, bricklayers, labourers, etc.; the women of Class B are frequently factory machinists. Intermediate and Skilled Non-manual work is equally open to men and women, as is reflected in Class E; and Classes C and D reflect the fact that some such occupations are essentially female (shop assistants, typists) or dominated by women (nursing, teaching). Again the Sex factor seems to be a manifestation of Social Class, except in the distinction between Classes A and B. Why should sex be a factor in the latter case? One can only speculate, wondering perhaps if women are more strongly influenced by the prestige dialect than their menfolk of the same Social Class. It appears that in southern France, for example, peasant women abandon Provençal dialect for standard French more readily than men; and that this can extend to features of pronunciation, the men using the apical trill for /r/ and the women the Parisian uvular fricative.

Social Class and Length of Schooling. This can be dealt with quite briefly: again we seem to have here a reflection of Social Class as the dominant factor. The division line is between Classes D and E, and

this is also where the change from Skilled Non-manual to Intermediate occupations occurs. (For statistical purposes we had to
amalgamate these two classes, but here they must be distinguished.)
Most Intermediate occupations involve some sort of training, usually
after extra years at school.

We may conclude, then, that Social Class is one of the strongest
influences on the speech of the informants, with Income Group, Sex
and Length of Schooling as subsidiary, but related factors. The other
major parameter which emerges as important from the survey results
in Place of Birth, but here the influence on linguistic classification
operates in a different way.

Class A is by far the largest linguistic category, containing nearly
half the informants interviewed. Members of this class speak in a
manner which closely approximates to the CUD standard, as
established in Chapter IV. One wonders what relationship there is
between CUD and other local accents of South Staffordshire. For
the urban areas there is no comparable statistical information; but
work has been done on the dialects of rural Staffordshire. In the
following chapter it will be shown that CUD does not differ markedly,
apart from a few points, from the speech of the rest of the county.
This suggests that we may take CUD as representing ' basic Cannock
speech', and the five linguistic classes (in the order A to E) as progressive deviations from it, in the direction of the prestige accent,
RP. It is now evident that, if one was born in Cannock Urban
District or elsewhere in South Staffordshire (and a majority of the
informants in each class were—see above, p. 77), then the higher up
the social scale one's occupation is considered to be, the more one's
speech is likely to be influenced by RP. Some may consider this
regrettable, but it is not particularly surprising.

It appears that the influence of occupational class is felt by indivi-
duals. The Place of Birth factor works differently. It has been noted
that in the higher-valued occupations (Intermediate and Skilled
Non-manual) people tend to move away from their home areas.
Few teachers, for example, are natives of the area in which their
school is situated. This accounts for the correlations between Linguistic Class and Social Class and between Linguistic Class and
Place of Birth: in Classes A and B we find mainly manual workers,
the people whose jobs do not normally cause them to change their
homes. Conversely, the reason why the proportion of locally-born
informants is lower in Classes D and E is not only that skilled

workers have moved away from Cannock but also that there has been an influx from outside the dsitrict. Even so, the effect is not so marked as one might have expected: even in Classes D and E, a sizeable majority of the informants were born and brought up in Cannock or South Staffordshire.

We will now look at the stages in the progressive deviation away from CUD in the direction of RP:

Class A. Members of this class speak almost 'pure' CUD, which is hardly surprising since a sub-group of this class was used to define CUD—see page 39. Informant no. 87 is the only one who was not born in Cannock or South Staffordshire, and both his parents were Staffordshire people. But the most noticeable feature of this class is that 27 of the 31 informants are men.

Class A to Class B. Very little change: only two informants were born outside the county, and most are Semi-skilled or Skilled Manual workers, although the proportion is lower in Class B than in Class A. But the balance of the sexes has now shifted sharply the other way: 16 of the 23 informants in Class B are women. The possible significance of this has been commented on above, p. 79.

Class B to Class C. In Class C the proportion of informants born in Cannock Urban District or elsewhere in South Staffordshire is much lower than in Classes A or B, but they still form a large majority. We have to be very cautious in drawing any conclusions from this or the two remaining classes, since none of them contain more than eight informants. Even so, it is clear that in Class C all but one of the informants is in an Intermediate or Skilled Non-manual occupation (a nurse, a clerk, a sales manager and two typists), so it seems that in this case Social Class is the discriminating factor.

Class C to Class D. Here again, all but two of the informants are in Intermediate or Skilled Non-manual occupations (a nurse, a secretary and two shop assistants) and are basically no different from the informants in Class C. The only distinguishing feature of Class D is that only a small majority (57%) of the informants were born in Cannock or South Staffordshire, compared with 71% in Class C.

Class D to Class E. All but two of the informants are in Intermediate or Skilled Non-manual occupations (two nurses, a company director, an optician,a clerk and a mines rescue superintendent)—in fact most of these are Intermediate occupations, and we have already seen (p. 80) that such occupations normally presuppose more than the minimum education. Whereas most informants in Classes A to D had left school as soon as was legally possible at the time, in Class E a small majority had stayed on at school, one for 1 year, two for 2 years, and two for 3 years. This might be the differentiating factor, but it is not possible to be certain, as two of the informants are Londoners by origin, which also strengthens the RP influence on this class.

The following table summarises the above information—changes in comparison with the previous class are italicised:

TABLE 23

Class A: Men in Skilled Manual or Semi-skilled occupations, with minimum education, a large majority born in Cannock or South Staffs.

Class B: Women in Skilled Manual or Semi-skilled occupations, with minimum education, a large majority born in Cannock or South Staffs.

Class C: *Men and women* in *Skilled Non-manual occupations*, with minimum education, a large majority born in Cannock or South Staffs.

Class D: Men and women in Skilled Non-manual occupations, with minimum education, a *small majority* born in Cannock or South Staffs.

Class E: Men and women in *Intermediate occupations*, with *more than the minimum education*, a small majority born in Cannock or South Staffs.

We are now in a position to compare progressive deviations from CUD speech in the direction of RP with changes in the background of the informants. The following table should be compared with Table 23 above and also with Table 18 on page 61:

TABLE 24

Linguistic class	Changes of linguistic features	Changes of background description
Class A	Almost 'pure' CUD	Men, Semi-skilled or Skilled Manual, minimum education, most born in Cannock.
Class B	/ĀR/, /H/, /Ĭ/, /U/–/Q/	Women, Semi-skilled or Skilled Manual, minimum education, most born in Cannock
Class C	/I/, /Ĕ/, /E/, /ER/	Men and women, Skilled Non-manual, minimum education, most born in Cannock.
Class D	/Q̄/, /Ō/, /O/, /Ou/, vowel + /R/	Men and women, Skilled Non-manual, minimum education, more than half born in Cannock.
Class E	/Ā/, /A/, /U/, laugh etc. (Almost 'pure' RP)	Men and women, Intermediate, extra education, more than half born in Cannock.

Here we can see that, in the lowest social classes, whereas the men tend to speak in a CUD manner, the women already seem to make some modifications in the direction of the prestige accent, in particular employing the RP distinction between /U/ and /Q/, and being more careful with /H/. Turning to the non-manual workers, we find that most of the vowels and diphthongs are altered, but the evidence suggests that back vowels are more resistant to change than front vowels. It is not clear why this should be—perhaps the fact that there is more physical space for variation in the front part of the mouth has something to do with it. Those informants who are engaged in Intermediate occupations and have received more than the minimum education have also altered the most open vowels, using the RP pronunciation of /A/ and /U/. They also tend to use /AR/ in laugh, dance and glass, but the occurrence of the velar nasal still follows the CUD pattern in most cases (see top of Table 18, p. 61).

All we are asserting here is that certain linguistic changes appear to accompany certain social changes—there are no grounds for assuming a cause-and-effect relationship in the *details* described above. It seems psychologically plausible that a person engaged in a particular occupation may feel constrained to speak in a certain way; that is a fact of general human experience. But we cannot say, for example, that Skilled Non-manual work changes people's vowel-sounds (in two stages) and that Intermediate occupations induce further alterations. That would be going beyond the evidence. What may be true is this: there are social pressures tending to produce alterations in speech in the direction of the prestige accent. The more highly valued by society one's occupation is, the stronger that pressure will be, and more changes in speech are likely to occur. There is a general order in which changes in pronunciation take place, in proportion to the strength of social pressure—but the factors that determine that order are presumably phonetic, not social.

It is a matter of common experience that members of the higher social classes tend to live in certain parts of towns. In view of the correlation between occupational class and linguistic class, we would expect to find this reflected in the geographical distribution of the informants. The 'elite' area of Cannock Urban District can be seen on Map 3 in squares 50, 51, 59, 60, 61, 67, 68 and 75. The informants who live in this area include two from Class E, two from Class D and three from Class C. A smaller area of the same type is formed by squares 28, 29 and 40; two of the informants living there are from Class E.

There are three main areas with concentrations of Class A informants: (1) squares 82, 83 and 87; (2) squares 79, 80, 81, 84, 85, 86, 88, 89, 90, 92 and 93; (3) squares 12, 13, 18, 19, 20, 31, 32, 33. All of these consist largely of either old terraced houses or modern council estates. Nineteen of the thirty-one Class A informants live in one of these three areas.

Summary

In the foregoing pages it has been shown that:
(a) It is possible to define a basic 'Cannock accent' (CUD), using as a basis the speech of those informants who were born in Cannock and have lived all their lives there;
(b) By comparing the speech of each informant with CUD on the

one hand and with RP on the other, one can sort the informants into five classes, *by purely linguistic criteria*.

(c) Fifty-four out of eighty informants have a majority of features in common with CUD.

(d) The changes of features of pronunciation from one linguistic class to the next are not haphazard, but form a clear progression; and this progression has points of contact with changes that have taken place in the history of the language.

(e) Age of informants is not a factor determining linguistic classification.

(f) Linguistic classification is influenced mainly by (1) the Place of Birth of the informants, and (2) a complex of the following factors: Income Group, Sex, Length of Schooling, Social Class, the latter being dominant.

Furthermore, it will be shown in Chapter VIII that Cannock speech does not differ radically from that of rural South Staffordshire.

CHAPTER VIII

A broader view

The approach adopted in this research (using a random sample of the electorate of a precisely defined area) has inevitably led us to treat Cannock Urban District as a kind of linguistic island, isolated from the surrounding area; though it has been necessary to point out several times that some of the immediately adjoining districts are linguistically related. The purpose of this final chapter is to broaden the scope a little, by looking at Cannock speech in relation to that of the rest of the County of Stafford, and the West Midlands in general.

For a description of the dialects of rural Staffordshire we rely on Peter H. Gibson's field-work for the *Survey of English Dialects*. His results are, of course, incorporated in the *West Midland Counties* volume of S.E.D., but his material was also written up into an unpublished thesis *Studies in the Linguistic Geography of Staffordshire*, submitted in 1955 for the M.A. degree of the University of Leeds. In the following paragraphs, page references are to the thesis.

Gibson studied the speech of a number of informants in twelve villages in various parts of Staffordshire. Those nearest to Cannock are Mavesyn Ridware (about 10 miles NNE), Lapley (5 miles W) and Himley (15 miles SW).

It should be borne in mind throughout what follows that Gibson's material and the Cannock survey are not strictly comparable. In the first place, one of the objects of S.E.D. was to record the rapidly disappearing ancient dialects of rural England; cf. Gibson, p. 37:

... the present survey has been undertaken only just in time to preserve the remaining dialect.

The emphasis is on historical evolution, and so in his chapters on phonology, Gibson presents the various vowels and diphthongs as reflexes of the Middle English vowels, rather than as realisations of Modern English phonemes, as is done in this book.

Again, the historical emphasis requires that informants should be speakers of pure dialect, and therefore elderly, uneducated people who have rarely, if ever, left their native village are chosen as informants. Gibson's youngest informant was fifty-eight at the time of his survey; his is therefore a description of the Staffordshire dialect of the turn of the century, rather than of the present time.

As already explained in Chapter I, this method, which is the appropriate way to investigate rural dialect, would be invalid if applied to an urban area. In any case, much of the material in the Dieth-Orton questionnaire which relates to the technicalities of farming, would be meaningless to the average town-bred citizen.

Nevertheless, having said all this, it will be useful to see what comparisons and contrasts, if any, can be made between Cannock Urban District and the surrounding area.

Gibson's work has shown that there is an important dialect boundary which crosses Staffordshire along the northern edge of the valley of the Trent (see especially his Chapter IV, pp. 195–283). The differences between the dialects of North and Mid-Staffordshire are primarily lexical although there are some phonetic distinctions also. (South Staffordshire, being predominantly urban, does not figure very largely in Gibson's work; Himley is the only village in this region.) Obviously we are here interested in making comparisons with the Mid-Staffordshire dialect.

About the Black Country, Gibson says (p. xxxiv):
It is apparent, even to the casual visitor, that the phonetic system of the Black Country differs fundamentally from that of either of the localities so far investigated in the neighbourhood of the Black Country.

We shall see that as far as Cannock, which lies at the edge of the Black Country, is concerned, this is an exaggeration. In the following table, the normal CUD realisations of the phonemes are compared with Gibson's Mid-Staffordshire results, taken from Chapters II and III of his thesis. /U/ does not appear, being identical with /Q/ in both systems.

TABLE 25

Phoneme	CUD	Mid-Staffordshire
/Ā/	[ɛɪ]	[ɛɪ]
/Ē/	[ɪ̈ɪ]	[iː]
/Ī/	[äɪ]	[ɒɪ]
/Ou/	[äɔ]	[æɔ]
/Q̄/	[ə̈ü]	[üː]
/Ō/	[ɔ̈ɔ]	[ɒɔ]
/Ū/	[jü]	[jü]
/Oi/	[ɔɪ]	[ɒɪ]
/A/	[a]	[a]
/E/	[ɛ]	[ɛ]
/I/	[ɪ̞]	[ɪ̞]
/Q/	[ɵ]	[ɵ]
/O/	[ɒ]	[ɒ]
/AR/	[ä:]	[a:]
/ER/	[ə̈:]	[ə:]
/OR/	[ɔ̈:]	[ɔ:]
/ĀR/	[ɛ:]	[ɛ:]
/ĒR/	[ɪ̈iə]	[ɪə]
/ĪR/	[äɪə]	[ɒɪə]
/OuR/	[äɔə]	[aɔə]

The first thing to notice is that there is little difference in the realisations of the short vowels, which is not surprising: long vowels and
diphthongs are generally subject to wider ranges of variation. In
seven cases there is absolute identity between CUD and Mid-
Staffordshire pronunciation, i.e. for /Ā/, /Ū/, /A/, /E/, /Q/, /O/ and
/ĀR/. (Four of these are short vowels.) In five other cases the
similarity is so close that what differences there are may be put down
to idiosyncratic differences between investigators; these are /Ou/,
/I/, /ER/, /OR/ and /OuR/. (Gibson's description on page 50 and
diagram on page 52 do not make it clear whether the Mid-Staffordshire realisation of /I/ is closer than that of RP or not; the CUD
realisation is noticeably closer.)

In the remaining eight cases there are notable differences between
CUD and Mid-Staffordshire vowels, which we will now discuss.

/Ē/ and /Ō/. According to Gibson, these are both pure vowels in
Mid-Staffordshire, whereas in CUD they are clearly diphthongal. In
fact, since RP also has diphthongal realisations of these phonemes,
nearly all the Cannock informants use diphthongs here. The CUD
diphthongs are, however, wider than those of RP; some informants
have an even broader diphthong for /Ē/: [əi], which has been

classified as CUD+. The only Cannock informants with pure-vowel realisations of these phonemes are those who originate in Scotland or on Tyneside, and who had to be excluded from the linguistic classification. It appears that in Cannock these phonemes are realised very differently from what is general in the county.

/Ī/ and /Oi/. In CUD these vowels are different; in Staffordshire dialect generally they are the same, i.e. there is one phoneme fewer. /Oi/ has been a diphthong since the Middle Ages—it generally occurs in words of French origin. /Ī/ was a pure long vowel [i:] in Middle English; it became a diphthong in the fifteenth century (Prins: *A History of English Phonemes*, p. 128) and the starting-point became more and more central, reaching [ʌɪ] in the eighteenth century. From there the starting-point moved forward in RP, to [äɪ], but backward in the West Midlands to CUD [ɑɪ] and Mid-Staffordshire (ɒɪ). The Mid-Staffordshire diphthong is used by some Cannock informants and we have classed it as CUD+; among older members of the community one can hear *oil*, *Joyce* and *boil* pronounced as 'ile', 'Jice' and 'bile', from which we observe that fusion of these two phonemes has not been unknown in Cannock. Perhaps it is RP influence, greater in a town, that has kept them generally apart, whereas they have merged in the rural parts of the county.

/Ō/. The Staffordshire diphthong is wider than that of CUD.

/AR/. This is certainly the most important difference between Staffordshire dialect and CUD. According to Gibson, the vowel in rural Staffordshire is approximately Cardinal 4 [a:], whereas in Cannock it is an advanced Cardinal 5 [ä:]. Again, since RP has the same realisation, this applies to nearly all Cannock informants. No examples of [a:] were found in the survey; a few informants had a retracted variety, but they were all Northerners. Not a single locally-born Cannock informant has the same vowel that Gibson describes for the rest of the county. We cannot suppose that CUD originally had Cardinal 4, but has been influenced by RP, because in that case we would expect some front-vowel realisations from locally-born speakers; and there are none—indeed, the only deviations from the CUD norm are by retraction to Cardinal 5 [ɑ:]. The explanation of this notable difference must therefore remain problematical.

/ĒR/. Here again there is a triphthong in CUD but a diphthong elsewhere in the county. This is consistent with this sequence being a 'compound' of /Ē/, which exhibits the same difference.

/Ī/. CUD has a different triphthong from rural Mid-Staffordshire in this sequence, just as it does for /Ĭ/.

We now turn our attention briefly to the consonants (for rural Staffordshire, see Gibson, pp. 74 and 75).

/H/ is missing from Staffordshire dialect, except in refined speech or in cases of hypercorrection. It has already been suggested that in CUD also the presence of /H/ is a symptom of RP influence.

Gibson states that /L/ is clear in Staffordshire dialects, except in Himley where it is dark . It is not clear whether he means that /L/ has the same quality in all positions. In Cannock, for all informants, the distribution of clear and dark /L/ is the same as in RP.

'Aspiration of the consonants *p*, *t* and *k* is not general' and only occurs in two localities in the far north of the county, and also at Lapley 'where slight aspiration of these consonants is heard both initially and finally' (Gibson, p. 75). In Cannock, however, voiceless plosives are normally strongly aspirated before stressed vowels, and also finally; they may even be affricated. Moreover, initial and final lenis plosives and fricatives are usually devoiced, at least partially; Gibson does not mention whether this occurs in rural Staffordshire or not. Aspiration of fortis plosives and devoicing of lenis obstruents are also characteristic of RP.

On pages 296 and 298 of his thesis, Gibson discusses briefly the ending -*ing* and the group NG in other contexts. His results agree with those of the Cannock survey that the G is normally pronounced; in cases where the velar nasal occurs alone, he ascribes it to RP influence.

In unstressed syllables, including present participles, the /NG/ group is usually reduced to /N/; in this context, velar nasals occur only occasionally, and these Gibson ascribes to either analogy or RP influence, on the historical ground that the inflexion of the present participle in Middle English was -*inde*. In CUD, on the other hand, [ŋ] is the usual pronunciation of /NG/ in unstressed syllables; only a very few informants gave examples of [n], and these by no means consistently.

The results of the Cannock survey can also usefully be compared with some of the material in J. C. Wells' article on 'Local accents in England and Wales' in the autumn 1970 edition of the *Journal of Linguistics*. His survey includes the West Midlands, and in the course of his article he makes a number of interesting comments on the principles involved.

Wells recognises that an *accent* is not the same as a dialect, but equally worthy of study:

> The vast mass of urban working-class and lower-middle-class speakers use a pronunciation nearer to RP, and lexical and grammatical forms much nearer to Standard English, than the archaic rural dialects recorded by the dialectologists. Yet their speech diverges in many ways from what is described as standard. (. . .) It is the task of anyone concerned with the description of these 'accents' of English to investigate whatever phonetic variables can be identified and to establish their correlation with the non-linguistic variable of age, social standing and education, and geographical provenance. (p. 231)

Wells' statements about the 'accent' of the West Midlands are summarised below, with comparisons with the Cannock results. Paragraph references are to his article.

(1) Words which have /ʌ/ in RP have /ʊ/ in the 'broad' local accent and /ə/ in the 'less broad' (2.1). As can be seen from Appendix II, Table 27, column *iv*, only nine Cannock informants lack the /U/-/Q/ opposition altogether; the majority do have this contrast (not always correctly used), although very few have the RP realisation of /U/.

(2) The diphthong /ɒɪ/ is missing in certain areas, where the incidence of /aɪ/ is extended to words such as *toy*, *voice* (homophonous with *tie*, *vice*). (2.6).
As we have already seen (p. 89) this is only found among a few elderly people in Cannock, but is characteristic of the dialects of rural Staffordshire.

(3) Concerning the sequence /NG/, Wells says that in the Midlands the /G/ is either always pronounced, or only prevocalically (4.2). In Cannock, the conditioning factor is stress, i.e. the G is pronounced after a stressed vowel (*finger*). See page 51 for more details.

(4) Wells refers to the acquisition of /h/ by people whose speech is very far from RP because it is 'a most powerful shibboleth for English speech'. (4.3). This is as true in Cannock as elsewhere.

(5) The use of /æ/ in *laugh*, *path*, *grass* and similar words is a feature of the Midlands and the North, and as it is known to be

non-standard, cases of hypercorrection are sometimes found (6.1). In Cannock, substitution of 'long A' (as it is usually called) can be heard from those local people who consciously attempt to 'improve' their speech. Only five of the eighty informants in the sample do this consistently (and two of these come from London, so it is probably natural to them); a rather larger number are inconsistent, which suggests that their natural habit is to use 'short A'.

(6) Wells comments on the closeness of /ɪ/ in the West Midlands. (7.1).

(7) '/ɔ/ is opener in the Midlands and North, cardinal 6 or opener.' (7.4). This is certainly a feature of the speech of most Cannock informants, secondary 5, /ɒ/, being a common realisation of /O/.

Wells has an interesting reference to an unpublished thesis by Hurford:

> Hurford's thesis concerns the speech of three generations in a Cockney family. His findings might be summarized by saying that the specifically Cockney features appear to increase generation by generation at the expense of RP-influenced features. This finding is at odds with the usual assumption that characteristic regional pronunciation features are, like rural dialects, generally dying out. It would be interesting to know whether, and to what extent, this is true of local urban speech away from London.

We have already quoted Professor Brook's remark on the same subject (above, p. 8). It is not possible, without going beyond the evidence, to give an unequivocal answer to this question, since we have no comparable material from different generations in one Cannock family; but one of the conclusions of the survey was that, in Cannock, there appears to be no correlation between the age of the informants and their speech-habits (Chapter VII, p. 75). There is no evidence that CUD is on the increase, but it is certainly not dying out.

Some morphological features

Gibson's Chapter V deals mainly with morphological features of the Staffordshire dialects, although he has little to say about these, in comparison with his exhaustive treatment of phonetics. The Cannock survey was restricted from the outset to phonetic features, and so there is scarcely any morphological material in the recordings. However the present writer, as a native of Cannock, feels able to point out some similarities to, and differences from, Gibson's findings.

It should be emphasized that the following descriptions of some features of Cannock morphology stem entirely from the writer's own knowledge, and *not* from the random sample of the electorate used in establishing the phonetic data. On the other hand, the features involved are characteristic of the speech of elderly locally-born people (without being by any means confined to them), and so are perhaps more comparable with Gibson's informants than those selected in the random sample.

Auxiliary verbs, especially negatives (see Gibson, pp. 291–3). Generally in Staffordshire, negative auxiliaries have disyllablic forms. Gibson quotes:

can't	= ['kanə]
won't	= ['wɒnə]
shouldn't	= ['ʃʊdnə]
mustn't	= ['mʊnə]

There are other variants, such as:

can't	= ['kɒnə]
wasn't	= ['wʌnə]

Forms like these can readily be heard in use, even by children, in central Staffordshire and the adjoining parts of Shropshire.

Himley is different from the rest of the county, since there either standard forms are found, or forms which lack the nasal consonant. Gibson quotes:

you aren't	= [joʊˈɛɪ]
there isn't	= [ðərˈɛɪ]

Cannock has no trace of the disyllabic negatives; the traditional local forms are similar to those found at Himley. They are probably normal in the Black Country and adjacent areas. More details are given below.

The verb 'to be'. The present tense affirmative shows a tendency to generalise *am* at the expense of *are*:

I am   = *I'm*   → [ä:m]
you are   = *you'm* → [jɔɒm]
we are   = *we'm* → [wɪ̭m]

In the negative this process is complete: only one verb-form appears, and the nasal consonant is missing, as at Himley:

I'm not   → *I ay*   = [äɪ ɛɪ]
you aren't   → *you say* = [jɔɒ ɛɪ]
he isn't   → *he ay*   = [ɪ̈i ɛɪ]
she isn't   → *her ay* = [ər ɛɪ]
we aren't   → *we ay*   = [wɪ̈i ɛɪ]
they aren't → *they ay* = [ðɛɪ ɛɪ]

The affirmative forms of the preterite are as in Standard English, but when negative the nasal consonant is again missing, and one verb-form does duty for all:

I wasn't   → *I wor*   = [ä: wɔ:]
you weren't → *you wor* = [jɔɒ wɔ:]
etc.

The verb 'to have'. The present tense is quite normal when affirmative, but the negative paradigm is identical with the negative of 'to be'. The preterite forms, affirmative and negative, are much as in Standard English, apart from differences of pronunciation.

The verb 'can'. The affirmative forms of both tenses are normal, but a single paradigm serves as both present and preterite in the negative. Again one verb-form is generalized, and there is no nasal element:

I can't   = *I couldn't*   → *I cor*   = [ä: kɔ:]
you can't = *you couldn't* → *you cor* = [jɔɒ kɔ:]
etc.

The verb 'to do'. Here again, only the negative forms require comment: the same features are found as with the other auxiliary verbs, and present and preterite forms as distinguished by a single vowel:

I don't   → *I dow*   = [ä: dɔɒ]
you don't → *you dow* = [jɔɒ dɔɒ]

he doesn't → *he dow* = [ˈi̯i dʒꭥ]
etc.

I didn't → *I day* = [ă: dɛɪ]
you didn't → *you day* = [jꭥ dɛɪ]
etc.

The verb 'will'. The negative of the present tense of this verb exhibits the usual phenomenon:

I won't → *I wow* = [ă: wʒꭥ]
you won't → *you wow* = [jꭥ wʒꭥ].

Other features

(1) The personal pronoun subject of the first person singular (*I*) appears in its full form ([ăɪ]) only before a vowel, as in *I ay* (for *I'm not*). Otherwise the diphthong is reduced to [ă:]. The latter is also the usual local equivalent of *yes*.

(2) Cannock speech agrees with that of the rest of the county in using *her* ([ə:]) as the subject pronoun of the third person singular feminine (instead of *she*).

(3) Another point of agreement with Gibson's results is the use of *as* as a relative pronoun. *What* is less commonly used.

(4) *Them* is commonly used as the plural of the demonstrative adjective and pronoun *that* (*them books*). Gibson does not mention this feature, but there is no reason to suppose it to be limited to this area.

None of the informants in the random sample spoke in quite the archaic manner just described, but one such speaker was found by chance. He is the husband of informant no. 10. As his accent was so interesting and easily available, he was interviewed in the same way as his wife, and in addition he was invited to record a conversation. This he willingly did; the conversation lasted about three-quarters of an hour, and consisted largely of his reminiscences of life in Hednesford (known locally as [ˈɛdʒfəd], see Map 2) in the early years of the century. For comparison with the informants in the survey, background information on this person is as follows:

He is of course a married man; he was seventy-nine years old at the time of the interview (early 1968); he was born in Hednesford and had spent all his life there. Both his parents were born in Oakengates in Shropshire (now part of Telford new town). He attended a 'C. of E. school' and left at the age of twelve. At one time he was apprenticed to a blacksmith; he was a miner for twenty-three years. He is now of course retired and living on his pension, his income being less than £500 per annum.

The following analysis of the features of his pronunciation should be compared with the description of Class A on p.64.

1. *Laugh*, *dance* and *glass* all have the vowel /A/. CUD.
2. *One* has the vowel /O/. CUD.
3. The /G/ is pronounced in *sing*, *singer* and *singing*. CUD.
4. The contrast between /U/ and /Q/ is completely missing; only /Q/ occurs. CUD.
5. Realisations of the sequence 'base vowel + /R/' are monophonemic. RP.
6. /H/ is missing. CUD.
7. /Ā/ = [ɛ̨ɩ] CUD+.
8. /Ē/ = [ə̣ɩ] CUD+.
9. /Ī/ = [ɑɩ] CUD+.
10. /Ou/ = [aω] CUD+.
11. /Q/ = [ə̣ü] CUD.
12. /Ō/ = [ɔω] CUD.
13. /Oi/ = [ɒ̈ɩ]
14. /A/ = [ä] CUD+.
15. /E/ = [ɛ] CUD.
16. /I/ = [ɩ̣] CUD.
17. /U/ is missing. CUD.
18. /Q/ = [ω] CUD.
19. /O/ = [ɒ̈] CUD+.
20. /AR/ = [ɑ:] CUD+.
21. /ER/ = [ɛ̣:] CUD+.
22. /OR/ = [ɒ̣:] CUD+.
23. /ĀR/ = [ɛ̣:] CUD.

Note on nos. 21 and 23: these phoneme sequences are identically realised in this gentleman's speech. He has a higher number of CUD+ features (there are nine of them) than any informant in the random sample: nos. 48 and 93 each have seven.

Appendix I

In this appendix the background information required from each informant has been tabulated. The material has been coded to make the tables as compact as possible. The only information not included here is the informant's occupation, which is dealt with in Chapter II.

The interpretation of the table is as follows:

1. Column A gives the sex of the informant: m = male; f = female.
2. Column B gives the marital status of the informant: m = married; s = single; w = widowed.
3. Column C gives the informant's age in 1968.
4. Column D gives the age at which the informant left school.
5. Column E gives the income group of the household as follows: a = £0–£499; b = £500–£999; c = £1000–£1499; d = £1500–£1999; e = £2000–£2499; f = £2500–£2999; g = £3000 or over.
6. Column F shows how the income is received: w = wages; s = salary; p = pension; e = self-employed.
7. Column G gives the birthplace of the informant's mother.
8. Column H gives the birthplace of the informant's father.
9. Column I gives the birthplace of the informant.
10. Column J gives the place where the informant lived most of the time up to the age of 11.
11. Column K gives the place where the informant lived most of the time between the ages of 11 and 18.
12. Column L gives the place where the informant has spent most of his or her life since the age of 18.
13. Column M gives any other place where the informant has lived

more than a year, excluding any military service. The number of years is given in brackets.

In columns G to M, the following symbols are used for places in the Urban District of Cannock. They are all shown on Map 3.

Bh	= Broomhill	HS	= Hazel Slade
Bl	= Blackfords	Lw	= Littleworth
Br	= Bridgtown	NC	= Norton Canes
Ca	= Cannock	NE	= Norton East
Cb	= Churchbridge	PG	= Pye Green
Ch	= Chadsmoor	PV	= Prospect Village
CW	= Cannock Wood	Ra	= Rawnsley
He	= Hednesford	Wi	= Wimblebury
Hi	= Hightown	WC	= West Chadsmoor
HH	= Heath Hayes		

Also in columns G to M, other places are shown with the following codes:

Ald	= Aldridge, Staffs.	L	= London
Ay	= Ayrshire	La	= Lancashire
B	= Birmingham	Lan	= Lanarkshire
Bre	= Brewood, Staffs.	Li	= Liverpool
Bro	= Brownhills, Staffs.	Lic	= Lichfield, Staffs.
Bt	= Bristol	M	= Manchester
Bur	= Burntwood, Staffs.	Mon	= Monmouthshire
Che	= Cheshire	Mt	= Montgomeryshire
CH	= Cheslyn Hay, Staffs.	N	= Newcastle-upon-Tyne
Db	= Derbyshire	Nb	= Northumberland
Den	= Denbighshire	Nt	= Nottinghamshire
Du	= Durham	NW	= North Wales
Dud	= Dudley, Worcs.	O	= Oxfordshire
Fi	= Fife	Pen	= Penkridge, Staffs.
G	= Glasgow	R	= Rutland
Gal	= Galway, Ireland	Rug	= Rugeley, Staffs.
Gib	= Gibraltar	Sa	= Shropshire
Gl	= Gloucestershire	Sr	= Surrey
Gla	= Glamorgan	St	= Staffordshire, excluding
GW	= Great Wyrley, Staffs.		places listed elsewhere.
Hun	= Huntington, Staffs.	Sta	= Stafford
J	= Jerusalem	Sx	= Sussex

Tam = Tamworth, Staffs.   Wa = Warwickshire
W   = Wiltshire   Wal = Walsall, Staffs.
                               Wol = Wolverhampton, Staffs.

For convenience the background information has been split into two parts, the information in columns A to F being presented in Table 26a, and columns G to M in Table 26b.

TABLE 26a

Informant No.	A	B	C	D	E	F
1	f	m	42	14	c	w
3	f	m	34	14	c	w
4	m	m	29	15	b	w
5	m	m	25	15	c	e
7	f	m	52	14	c	w
8	f	m	61	14	a	p
9	m	m	26	15	b	w
10	f	m	79	12	a	p
11	m	m	51	14	c	w
12	f	m	32	15	c	w
13	m	m	67	13	a	p
14	f	m	26	15	b	w
15	f	s	33	15	b	w
16	f	m	43	14	b	s
18	f	m	33	16	c	s
19	m	m	38	14	b	w
20	m	m	63	13	b	s
21	m	m	62	13	c	w
22	m	m	60	13	b	w
23	f	m	24	15	b	w
25	m	m	32	15	c	s
26	m	m	58	14	c	w
28	f	m	67	15	b	p
29	m	m	38	16	d	w
30	m	m	46	14	c	w
31	m	m	41	14	c	w
33	m	m	70	13	a	p
34	m	w	55	14	b	w
35	m	m	26	17	c	s
36	m	m	23	15	b	w
37	f	w	70	14	a	p
38	f	m	52	14	c	w
39	m	m	56	14	c	w
40	m	m	31	15	e	e
41	f	m	53	14	c	w

TABLE 26a (*cont*).

Informant No.	A	B	C	D	E	F
42	f	w	68	13	a	p
43	m	m	54	14	—	e
44	m	m	65	13	b	w
45	m	m	43	14	c	w
46	m	m	39	17	e	s
48	f	m	39	14	b	w
49	m	m	49	14	c	w
50	m	m	38	17	f	s
51	m	m	51	17	g	s
52	f	m	61	13	—	—
53	m	m	38	14	b	w
54	f	m	31	15	c	w
55	f	m	25	15	c	w
56	f	m	73	13	b	p
57	f	m	46	14	c	w
60	f	w	68	16	—	—
61	f	m	45	15	b	w
62	m	m	61	13	b	w
63	f	m	25	15	—	—
64	f	m	47	14	b	w
65	f	m	67	14	c	s
66	f	m	63	13	a	p
67	f	m	28	15	b	w
68	f	m	53	14	c	e
69	m	m	42	14	c	w
71	m	m	54	14	c	w
72	f	m	36	14	b	s
73	m	m	53	14	b	w
74	m	m	31	15	b	w
75	m	m	44	14	c	w
76	f	m	32	15	c	w
77	f	m	50	14	c	s
78	m	m	38	14	c	s
80	m	m	43	14	c	w
82	m	m	47	14	c	w
83	f	m	68	12	a	p
84	m	m	46	14	b	w
85	m	m	57	14	b	w
86	m	m	76	14	a	p
87	m	w	66	13	a	p
88	m	m	26	15	b	w
89	m	m	56	14	b	w
91	f	m	29	18	c	s
92	m	m	39	14	d	e
93	f	m	36	14	c	w

TABLE 26b

(Places in the Urban District are underlined.)

Informant No.	G	H	I	J	K	L	M
1	Wal	Wal	PG	PG	PG	PG	—
3	NW	?	Ca	Ca	Ca	Ca	PG(5)
4	Ca	O	Ca	Ca	Ca	Ca	PG(3½)
5	He	He	Ch	Ch	Ch	He	—
7	He	He	Ra	Ra	Ra	He	—
8	?	He	He	He	He	He	Wal(4)
9	Wal	Wal	Wol	Wol	Wol	Wol	Ca(4)
10	Gl	Sa	He	He	He	He	B(5)
11	Dud	B	Ra	Ra	St	Ra	Che(4); St(4)
12	N	N	N	N	N	Ca	—
13	Ch	He	WC	WC	WC	WC	—
14	He	HS	He	He	He	He	—
15	Wal	Wal	Wal	He	He	He	Sa(3½); Gib(2); Sr(1)
16	Mon	L	L	L	L	Ra	He(2); HS(5)
18	Dud	Mon	Dud	Dud	Dud	Dud	CW(3)
19	He	He	Ch	Ch	Ch	Ch	—
20	He	He	He	He	He	He	—
21	Wal	Sa	WC	WC	WC	J	Hi(20)
22	Lic	Wol	HS	HS	HS	HS	He(1)
23	Ca	CH	Ca	Ca	Br	He	—
25	Ch	He	He	Bh	Bh	Ca	Bur(2½); He(1½)
26	Lic	Lic	Lic	Ra	Ra	Ra	—
28	Sx	Bur	Bur	Bur	Bur	Bur	Bre(9); Wa(2); CW(1)
29	Dud	Tam	B	Fi	Wa	B	Wa(4); CW(5)
30	Pen	Wol	St	Ca	Ca	Ca	—
31	Nb	Nb	Nb	Nb	Nb	Nb	Ca(5½)
33	Wal	Sta	Ch	Ch	Ch	Ch	—
34	Bro	Lic	Du	Du	Bro	Ca	—
35	He	HS	He	Ch	He	He	—
36	He	He	He	He	He	He	—
37	Wal	Rug	Bur	Bur	Lw	Lw	—
38	Bur	Br	Br	Br	GW	Wi	He(10); St(1½)
39	Wal	Nb	Bur	Bur	Bur	PV	—
40	HH	NC	HH	HH	HH	CW	—
41	?	La	Che	La	La	Sta	Ca(3)
42	HH	Wal	Wal	Wal	Wal	HH	B(2)
43	Li	Wol	Bl	Bl	Bl	Bl	—
44	Cb	Wal	Cb	Cb	Cb	Ca	—
45	Wol	Wol	He	He	He	He	—
46	He	Wa	He	He	He	He	Ca(7)
48	Wi	Bur	HS	HS	HS	HS	Rug(1½); Wi(4)

TABLE 26b (cont.)

Informant

No.	G	H	I	J	K	L	M
49	NC	Ca	Ca	Ca	Ca	Wi	—
50	Wol	W	Wol	Wol	Wol	Wol	Ca(5)
51	Gal	Wal	Wal	Wal	Wol	Ca	—
52	?	Wol	Br	Br	Br	Ca	—
53	Lan	G	G	G	G	G	Ca(3)
54	Hi	Ch	Hi	Hi	Hi	Hi	Ca(5)
55	Wal	GW	GW	Wal	GW	GW	Ca(2)
56	Bro	Bro	Bro	Bro	HH	HH	NC(2)
57	?	B	B	B	B	B	HH(3)
60	Wa	?	Pen	Pen	Pen	Ca	Dud(3); Wol(3)
61	Sa	St	Sa	Sa	Mt	Ca	Li(2); M(2)
62	M	Den	He	He	He	He	Ca(28)
63	Pen	GW	GW	GW	GW	Ca	GW(3)
64	Bro	Bro	Bro	Bro	Bro	HH	—
65	Sa	Ra	Lw	Lw	Lw	HH	Ch(5); Db(1½); Rug(1)
66	NC	GW	NC	NC	HH	HH	—
67	Bl	Hi	WC	WC	WC	Ca	He(3)
68	Ald	Dud	Gla	Dud	Ca	Ca	—
69	W	Rug	Ca	Ca	Ca	Ca	—
71	NE	GW	Bl	Bl	Bl	Ca	Hun(3)
72	Nt	Nt	Db	Sta	Sta	HH	Sta(6)
73	HH	NC	HH	HH	HH	HH	Ca(2); NC(2)
74	HH	Bur	Bur	Bur	Bur	HH	—
75	Ay	Ay	Ay	Ay	Ay	Ay	Ca(4½)
76	Wol	GW	Br	Ca	Ca	Ca	He(2)
77	Bt	Bt	Mon	Mon	Bt	Mon	Ca(9)
78	Ca	Ca	Ca	Ca	Ca	Ca	—
80	Wal	NC	NC	NC	NC	NC	—
82	L	L	L	L	L	Ca	—
83	Pen	St	Pen	Pen	Ch	Br	B(3); Ca(4)
84	NC	Bur	Bur	Nt	Bro	NC	CW(2)
85	Bro	NC	NC	NC	NC	NC	—
86	Li	Li	Li	Li	Li	Li	NC(27)
87	St	St	La	La	St	St	Ca(5)
88	Bur	Bur	NC	NC	NC	NC	—
89	Bur	R	Bur	Bur	Bur	NC	—
91	Wal	Bre	Ca	Wal	Wal	Wal	NC(4)
92	Wal	Dud	NC	NC	Bro	NC	Wal(3); Bur(3)
93	Bur	NC	Bur	NC	NC	NC	—

Appendix II

This appendix gives details of the twenty-three features of pronunciation used in setting up the linguistic classification of the informants. For each informant the phonetic realisation of each feature is listed and categorised as *RP+*, *RP*, *ble*. (short for *blend*), *CUD* or *CUD+*; or, in exceptionally difficult cases is left unassigned. The meaning of the categories is explained in Chapter V.

TABLE 27

This table lists the relevant *differences of incidence* and the *phonemic differences*.

Column *i* gives the phoneme, /A/ or /AR/, occurring in *laugh*, *dance* and *glass*. Cases of inconsistency are marked *f* (for fluctuation) —it means that two of the words had /A/ and the third /AR/, or vice versa.

Column *ii* gives the phoneme /U/ or /O/, occurring in *one*.

Column *iii* indicates whether the /NG/ sequence is realised according to the RP rule (*p*) or the CUD rule (*m*). Cases where the informant is inconsistent, e.g. no. 13 who pronounces *sing* with [g] but *singer* without, are marked *f*.

Column *iv* indicates whether the contrast betwee /U/ and /Q/ is present or missing. Again there are cases of fluctuation, marked *f*: some informants have the contrast but make mistakes by RP standards, e.g. no. 7 pronounces *pudding* with /U/ (ultracorrection) and no. 9 pronounces *bud* with /Q/.

Column *v* indicates whether the sequence 'base vowel phoneme + /R/' is to be regarded as a single phoneme (*1*) or as a sequence of two (*2*).

Column *vi* indicates whether the phoneme /H/ is present or missing.

In more complicated cases, an asterisk is entered in the table and a note added at the end.

TABLE 27

Informant No.	*i*	*ii*	*iii*	*iv*	*v*	*vi*
1	/A/ CUD	/U/ RP	m CUD	p RP	1 RP	m CUD
3	/A/ CUD	/U/ RP	*	p RP	1 RP	p RP
4	/A/ CUD	/O/ CUD	f ble.	m CUD	2 CUD	p RP
5	/A/ CUD	/O/ CUD	m CUD	p RP	1 RP	m CUD
7	/A/ CUD	/U/ RP	m CUD	f ble	2 CUD	p RP
8	/A/ CUD	/O/ CUD	m CUD	p RP	2 CUD	p RP
9	/A/ CUD	/O/ CUD	m CUD	f ble.	2 CUD	m CUD
10	/A/ CUD	/U/ RP	m CUD	f ble.	2 CUD	m CUD
11	f ble.	/O/ CUD	m CUD	p RP	1 RP	p RP
12	/A/ CUD	/O/ CUD	p RP	*	2 CUD	p RP
13	/A/ CUD	/O/ CUD	m CUD	m CUD	1 RP	m CUD
14	f ble.	/O/ CUD	m CUD	p RP	2 CUD	p RP
15	/A/ CUD	/O/ CUD	p RP	p RP	1 RP	p RP
16	/AR/ RP	/U/ RP	p RP	p RP	1 RP	p RP
18	f ble.	/O/ CUD	m CUD	p RP	1 RP	p RP
19	/A/ CUD	/O/ CUD	m CUD	m CUD	1 RP	m CUD
20	/A/ CUD	/O/ CUD	m CUD	*	1 RP	p RP
21	f ble.	/O/ CUD	m CUD	m CUD	1 RP	p RP
22	f ble.	/O/ CUD	m CUD	m CUD	2 CUD	m CUD
23	/A/ CUD	/O/ CUD	m CUD	p RP	1 RP	p RP
25	/A/ CUD	/O/ CUD	m CUD	p RP	2 CUD	p RP
26	/A/ CUD	/U/ RP	m CUD	f ble.	1 RP	m CUD
28	/AR/ RP	/U/ RP	m CUD	p RP	1 RP	p RP
29	/AR/ RP	/O/ CUD	m CUD	p RP	1 RP	p RP
30	/A/ CUD	/O/ CUD	m CUD	m CUD	1 RP	m CUD
31	/A/ CUD	/O/ CUD	p RP	p RP	1 RP	p RP
33	/A/ CUD	/O/ CUD	m CUD	p RP	2 CUD	m CUD
34	/A/ CUD	/O/ CUD	m CUD	f ble.	1 RP	p RP
35	/A/ CUD	/O/ CUD	m CUD	p RP	2 CUD	p RP
36	/A/ CUD	/U/ RP	m CUD	f ble.	2 CUD	p RP
37	/A/ CUD	/O/ CUD	m CUD	p RP	2 CUD	p RP
38	f ble.	/U/ RP	p RP	p RP	1 RP	p RP
39	/AR/ RP	/O/ CUD	m CUD	f ble.	1 RP	m CUD
40	/A/ CUD	/O/ CUD	m CUD	p RP	2 CUI	m CUD
41	f ble.	/U/ RP	m CUD	f ble.	*	p RP
42	/A/ CUD	/O/ CUD	m CUD	p RP	2 CUD	p RP
43	/A/ CUD	/O/ CUD	m CUD	p RP	2 CUD	p RP
44	/A/ CUD	*	m CUD	f ble.	2 CUD	m CUD

TABLE 27 (*cont.*)

Informant No.	i		ii		iii		iv		v		vi	
45	/A/	CUD	/O/	CUD	m	CUD	p	RP	2	CUD	p	RP
46	/AR/	RP	/U/	RP	m	CUD	p	RP	1	RP	p	RP
48	/A/	CUD	/O/	CUD	m	CUD	*		2	CUD	m	CUD
49	/A/	CUD	*		m	CUD	f	ble.	2	CUD	p	RP
50	/A/	CUD	/O/	CUD	p	RP	p	RP	2	CUD	p	RP
51	/AR/	RP	/U/	RP	m	CUD	p	RP	2	CUD	p	RP
52	/A/	CUD	/O/	CUD	m	CUD	p	RP	2	CUD	p	RP
53	/A/	CUD	/U/	RP	p	RP	p	RP	*		p	RP
54	/A/	CUD	/U/	RP	m	CUD	p	RP	2	CUD	p	RP
55	/A/	CUD	/O/	CUD	m	CUD	p	RP	1	RP	p	RP
56	/A/	CUD	/U/	RP	m	CUD	f	ble.	2	CUD	m	CUD
57	f	ble.	/O/	CUD	m	CUD	p	RP	2	CUD	p	RP
60	f	ble.	/O/	CUD	m	CUD	p	RP	1	RP	p	RP
61	/A/	CUD	/O/	CUD	m	CUD	p	RP	1	RP	p	RP
62	/A/	CUD	/O/	CUD	m	CUD	p	RP	1	RP	p	RP
63	/A/	CUD	/O/	CUD	m	CUD	f	ble.	1	RP	p	RP
64	/A/	CUD	/O/	CUD	m	CUD	f	ble.	2	CUD	m	CUD
65	f	ble.	/U/	RP	f	ble.	p	RP	1	RP	m	CUD
66	/A/	CUD	/O/	CUD	m	CUD	p	RP	2	CUD	m	CUD
67	/A/	CUD	/U/	RP	m	CUD	f	ble.	2	CUD	p	RP
68	f	ble.	/O/	CUD	m	CUD	p	RP	1	RP	p	RP
69	/A/	CUD	/O/	CUD	f	ble.	p	RP	1	RP	p	RP
71	/A/	CUD	/O/	CUD	m	CUD	f	ble.	2	CUD	m	CUD
72	/A/	CUD	/U/	RP	m	CUD	p	RP	2	CUD	p	RP
73	/A/	CUD	/O/	CUD	m	CUD	f	ble.	2	CUD	m	CUD
74	/A/	CUD	/U/	RP	m	CUD	p	RP	1	RP	p	RP
75	/A/	CUD	/U/	RP	p	RP	p	RP	*		p	RP
76	/A/	CUD	/U/	RP	f	ble.	p	RP	2	CUD	p	RP
77	*		/U/	RP	p	RP	p	RP	1	RP	p	RP
78	/A/	CUD	/O/	CUD	m	CUD	f	ble.	2	CUD	m	CUD
80	/A/	CUD	/Q/	RP	m	CUD	f	ble.	1	RP	m	CUD
82	/A/	CUD	/U/	RP	p	RP	p	RP	1	RP	p	RP
83	/A/	CUD	/O/	CUD	m	CUD	f	ble.	1	RP	p	RP
84	/A/	CUD	/U/	RP	m	CUD	m	CUD	2	CUD	m	CUD
85	/A/	CUD	/O/	CUD	m	CUD	*		2	CUD	m	CUD
86	/A/	CUD	/U/	RP	m	CUD	p	RP	2	CUD	m	CUD
87	/A/	CUD	/O/	CUD	m	CUD	f	ble.	2	CUD	m	CUD
88	/A/	CUD	/U/	RP	m	CUD	m	CUD	1	RP	m	CUD
89	/A/	CUD	/U/	RP	m	CUD	m	CUD	2	CUD	m	CUD
91	/A/	CUD	/O/	CUD	f	ble.	p	RP	2	CUD	p	RP
92	/A/	CUD	/O/	CUD	m	CUD	p	RP	2	CUD	m	CUD
93	/A/	CUD	/O/	CUD	m	CUD	f	ble.	1	RP	m	CUD

Notes on Table 27

Informant No.	Column No.	
3	iii	/G/ is deleted even in *finger* = [fɪŋə]. RP. The informant has a slight Welsh lilt.
12	iv	The vowel of *bud, dull* and *rubber* is the same as that of *girl, Bert* and *bird*. Unassignable. This informant has a distinctive Tyneside accent with a phonological system very different from either RP or CUD.
20	iv	*Bud* has /Q/ for /U/; the vowel of *dull* is very close to /Q/. Elsewhere /U/ is present where expected. This is taken to be an influence of the prestige dialect. ble.
41	v	Base vowel + /R/ is different from both RP and CUD—the post-vocalic /R/ is pronounced. Unassignable.
44	ii	The word *one* was not recorded.
48	iv	/U/–/Q/ contrast is generally absent, but *bud* and *dull* have a vowel [ɤ̆]. ble.
49	ii	The word *one* was not recorded.
53	v	Base vowel + /R/ is different from both RP and CUD—the post-vocalic /R/ is pronounced. Unassignable. This informant has a clear Scots accent.
75	v	See No. 53 v.
77	i	*Laugh, glass* have /A/, but *dance* appears to have /U/, the same vowel as in *dull, bud* and *rubber* Unassignable. This informant has a clear Welsh accent, with the typical intonation.
80	ii	As the /U/–/Q/ contrast is possibly not natural (see column *iv*) this is considered to be an RP pronunciation.
85	iv	/U/–/Q/ contrast is generally absent, but butter has a vowel [ɤ̆]. ble.

TABLE 28

This table gives the phonetic realisations of the vowel phonemes for each informant. As with the previous table, any difficult cases are marked with an asterisk and a note added at the end. As there are seventeen columns needed, the table is given in three parts.

Part 1

Informant No.	/Ā/	/Ē/	/Ī/	/Ou/	/Q̄/	/Ō/	/Oi/
1	[ɛɩ] CUD	[ɩ̜̈i] CUD	[äɩ] RP	[äω] CUD	[ə̣̌ü] CUD	[əω] RP	[ɔ̣ɩ] CUD
3	[ɛɩ] CUD	*	[äɩ] RP	*	[ωu] RP	[ɔ̣̈ω] ble.	[ɒ̣ɩ]
4	[ɛɩ] CUD+	[ɩ̜̈i] CUD	[ɑ̈ɩ] CUD	[ạω] CUD+	[ə̣ü] CUD	[ɔ̜ω] CUD	[ɔ̣ɩ] CUD
5	[ɛɩ] CUD	[ə̣ɩ] CUD+	[ɑ̈ɩ] CUD	[ạω] CUD+	[ə̣ü] CUD	[ɔ̜ω] CUD	[oɩ] RP+
7	[ɛ̜ɩ] CUD+	[ɩi] RP	[ɑ̈ɩ] CUD	[äω] CUD	[ʉ̜u] ble.	[ɔ̜̈ω] ble.	[ɔ̜ɩ] RP
8	[ɛ̜ɩ] CUD+	[ɩ̜̈i] CUD	[äɩ] RP	[ɑ̈ω] RP	[ʉ̜u] ble.	[ɔ̜ω] CUD	[ɔ̣ɩ] CUD
9	[ɛɩ] CUD	[ɩ̜̈i] CUD	[ɑɩ] CUD+	[äω] CUD	[əʉ̜] CUD	[ɔ̜ω] CUD	[ɒɩ]
10	[ɛɩ] CUD	[ɩ̜̈i] CUD	[ɑɩ] CUD+	[äω] CUD	[ωu] RP	[ɒ̣ω] CUD +	[ɔɩ] RP
11	[ɛ̣ɩ] ble.	[ɩi] RP	[ɑ̈ɩ] CUD	[ɑω] RP+	[ωü] ble.	[ɔω] CUD	[ɔɩ] RP
12	*	[i:]	*	[æu̜]	[u:]	[o̜:]	*
13	[ɛ̜ɩ] CUD+	[ɩi] RP	[ɑ̈ɩ] CUD	[äω] CUD	[ɨ̇ü] CUD	[ɔω] CUD	[ɔ̜̈ɩ]
14	[ɛɩ] CUD	[ɩ̜̈i] CUD	[ɑ̈ɩ] CUD	[äω] CUD+	[ə̣ü] CUD	[ɐω] RP+	[ɔ̣ɩ] CUD
15	[ɛɩ] CUD	*	*	[äω] CUD	[ə̣ü] CUD	[ɒω] CUD+	[ɔ̣ɩ] CUD
16	[ɛɩ] CUD	[ɩi] RP	[äɩ] RP	[aω] CUD+	[ə̣ü] CUD	[ɐω] RP+	[ɔɩ] RP
18	[ɛɩ] CUD	[ɩ̜̈i] CUD	[äɩ] RP	[äω] CUD	[ωu] RP	[ɔ̜̣ω] RP+	[ɔɩ] RP
19	[ɛ̜ɩ] CUD+	[əi] CUD+	[ɑ̈ɩ] CUD	[äω] CUD	[ə̣ü] CUD	[ɔ̜ω] CUD	[ɔɩ] RP
20	[ɛ̜ɩ] CUD+	[ɩ̜̈i] CUD	[ɑɩ] CUD+	[aω] CUD+	[ə̣ü] CUD	[ɔ̜̈ω] ble.	[ɔ̣ɩ] CUD
21	[ɛ̣ɩ] ble.	[ɩ̜̈i] CUD	[ɑ̈ɩ] CUD	[ɑ̈ω] RP	[ωu] RP	[ɔ̜̈ω] ble.	[ɔ̣ɩ] CUD
22	[ɛ̜ɩ] CUD+	[əi] CUD+	[ɒɩ] CUD+	[ɔ̜̽ω] CUD	[ə̜ü] CUD	[ɔ̜̈ω] ble.	[ɔɩ] RP

TABLE 28, Part 1 (cont.)

Informant No.	/Ā/	/Ē/	/Ī/	/Ou/	/Q̱/	/Ō/	/Oi/
23	[ɛι] CUD	[əi] CUD+	[äι] RP	[äω] CUD	[əü] CUD	[ʁω] RP+	[ɔι] CUD
25	[ɛι] CUD	[ui] RP	[äι] RP	[äω] CUD	[ʮu] ble.	[ọ̈ω] ble.	[ɔι] RP
26	[ęι] CUD+	[ui] RP	*	[aω] CUD+	*	[ɔ̈ω] ble.	[ɔ̧ι] CUD
28	[ęι] RP	[i̧:]	[äι] RP	[äω] RP	[ʁ:]	[əω] RP	[ɔ̧ι] RP
29	[ɛι] ble.	[ui] RP	[äι] RP	[aω] CUD+ble.	[ωü]	[əω] RP	[ɔ̧ι] CUD
30	[ęι] CUD+	[ÿi] CUD	[äι] CUD	[äω] CUD	[əü] CUD	[ɔω] CUD	[ɒι]
31	[ęι] RP	[i̧:]	[äι] CUD	[äü] CUD	[u:]	[ɛ̈ω] RP+	[ɔ̧ι] CUD
33	[ęι] CUD+	[ui] RP	[äι] RP	[aω] RP+	[ωu] RP	[ɔω] CUD	[ɒ̧ι]
34	[ęι] CUD+	[ÿi] CUD	[äι] CUD	[aω] CUD+	[ü]	[ʁ̧ω] CUD	[ö̧ι]
35	[ęι] CUD+	[ÿi] CUD	[äι] CUD	[äω] CUD	[ʮu] ble.	[ɔ̈ω] ble.	[ɔι] RP
36	[ɛι] CUD	[ÿi] CUD	[äι] CUD	[aʮ] CUD+	[əü] CUD	[ɔω] CUD	[ɔ̈ι]
37	[ęι] ble.	[ui] RP	[äι] RP	[äω] CUD	[əü] CUD	[ɒω] CUD	[ɔ̧ι] CUD
38	[ɛι] CUD	[ÿi] CUD	[äι] RP	[äω] RP	[ʮü] ble.	[ʁ̧ω] RP+	[ɔι] RP
39	[ɛι] CUD	*	*	[aω] CUD+	[əü] CUD	[ʁ̧ω] CUD	[ɔ̧ι] CUD
40	[ɛι] CUD	*	[äι] CUD	[aω] CUD+	[əü] CUD	[ɔ̈ω] ble.	[ɔι] RP
41	[ɛι] CUD	[ui] RP	[äι] RP	[äω] CUD	*	[ɔω] CUD	[ɔ̧ι] CUD
42	[ęι] CUD+	[ÿi] CUD	[aι] RP+	[aω] CUD+	[əü] CUD	[ɔ̈ω] ble.	[ɔ̧ι] RP
43	[ɛι] CUD	[ui] RP	[äι] CUD	[aω] CUD+	[əü] CUD	[ɔ̈ω] ble.	[ɔ̧ι] CUD
44	[ɛι] CUD	[ui] RP	*	[äω] RP	[ʮu] ble.	[ɔ̈ω] ble.	[ɔ̧ι] CUD
45	[ɛι] CUD	[ui] RP	[äι] CUD	[äω] CUD	[əü] CUD	[ɔ̈ω] ble.	[ɔ̧ι] CUD
46	[ęι] RP	[ui] RP	[äι] RP	[äω] CUD	[ωu] RP	*	[ɔ̧ι] CUD
48	[ęι] CUD+	[əi] CUD+	[ɒι] CUD+	[aω] CUD+	[əü] CUD	[ɒω] CUD+	[ɔ̧ι] RP

TABLE 28, Part 1 (*cont.*)

Informant No.	/Ā/	/Ē/	/Ī/	/Ou/	/Q̄/	/O/	/Oi/
49	[ɛ̞ɪ]	[ɪ̈i]	[äɪ]	[äɷ]	[ɞü]	[ɔɷ]	[ɔɪ]
	CUD+	CUD	CUD	CUD	ble.	CUD	RP
50	[ɛɪ]	[ɪ̞i]	*	[aɷ]	[ɘu]	[ɔ̆ɔ]	[ɒ̞ɪ]
	CUD	ble.		CUD+	ble.	ble.	RP
51	[ɛɪ]	[ui]	[äɪ]	*	[ɘu]	[ɐɷ]	[ɒ̞ɪ]
	CUD	RP	CUD		ble.	RP+	RP
52	[ɛɪ]	[ü̞i]	[äɪ]	[aɷ]	[ɘü]	[ɘɔ]	[ɒ̞ɪ]
	CUD	CUD	RP	CUD+	CUD	RP	RP
53	[ɛ̞:]	[i:]	[ɐɪ]	[äü]	[ʏ:]	[o:]	[ɒ̞ɪ]
				CUD			CUD
54	[ɛ̞ɪ]	[ë̞ɪ]	*	[aɷ]	[ɘü]	[äɷ]	[ɒ̞ɪ]
	CUD+	CUD		CUD+	CUD	RP+	RP
55	[ɛɪ]	[ɪ̞i]	[äɪ]	[aɷ]	[ɘü]	[ɔ̈ɷ]	[ɒ̞ɪ]
	CUD	CUD	RP	CUD+	CUD	ble.	
56	[ɛɪ]	[ui]	[äɪ]	[aɷ]	[ʉu]	[ɔɷ]	[ɔ̈ɪ]
	CUD	RP	RP+	CUD+	ble.	CUD	
57	[ɛ̞ɪ]	[ui]	[äɪ]	[äɷ]	[ü:]	[ë̞ɷ]	[ɒ̞ɪ]
	RP	RP	RP	CUD		RP+	RP
60	[ɛ̞ɪ]	[ui]	[aɪ]	[äɷ]	[ɘu]	[ɘɷ]	[ɒ̞ɪ]
	ble.	RP	RP+	CUD	ble.	RP	CUD
61	[ɛ̞ɪ]	[ui]	[äɪ]	[äɷ]	[ɘu]	[ɔ̈ɷ]	[ɒ̞ɪ]
	ble.	RP	RP	RP	ble.	ble.	RP
62	[ɛ̞ɪ]	[ui]	[äɪ]	[äɷ]	[ɘü]	[ɔ̈ɷ]	[ɒ̞ɪ]
	CUD+	RP	RP	RP	CUD	ble.	
63	[ɛ̞ɪ]	[ui]	[äɪ]	[äɷ]	[ɘü]	[ɘɷ]	[ɒ̞ɪ]
	RP	RP	RP	CUD	CUD	RP	CUD
64	[ɛɪ]	[ui]	*	[äɷ]	[ɘü]	[ɒɷ]	[ɒ̞ɪ]
	CUD	RP		CUD	CUD	CUD+	RP
65	[ɛ̞ɪ]	[ui]	*	[äɷ]	[ɞu]	[ɞ̞ɷ]	[ɒ̞ɪ]
	RP	RP		RP	RP	RP+	RP
66	[ɛ̞ɪ]	[ɪ̞i]	[äɪ]	[aɷ]	[ɘü]	[ɐ̞ɷ]	[ɒ̞ɪ]
	RP	CUD	RP	CUD+	CUD	RP+	CUD
67	[ɛɪ]	[ui]	[ɐɪ]	[äɷ]	[ɘü]	[ɐɷ]	[ɞ̞ɪ]
	CUD	RP	RP+	CUD	CUD	RP+	
68	[ɛ̞ɪ]	[ui]	[aɪ]	[aɷ]	[ɪ̞ü]	[ɐɷ]	[ɒ̞ɪ]
	RP	RP	RP+	CUD+	ble.	RP+	RP
69	[ɛ̞ɪ]	[ɪ̞i]	[äɪ]	[aɷ]	[ɘü]	[ɔɷ]	[ɒ̞ɪ]
	ble.	CUD	CUD+	CUD+	CUD	CUD	CUD
71	[ɛɪ]	[ɪ̞i]	[aɪ]	[äɷ]	[ɘü]	[ɞ̞ɷ]	[ɒ̞ɪ]
	CUD	CUD	CUD+	CUD	CUD	CUD	RP
72	[ɛɪ]	[ui]	[äɪ]	[äɷ]	[ʉu]	[ɔɷ]	[ɒ̞ɪ]
	CUD	RP	RP	RP	ble.	CUD	CUD
73	[ɛ̞ɪ]	[ɪ̈i]	[äɪ]	[äɷ]	[ʉu]	[ɔ̈ɷ]	[ɞ̞ɪ]
	ble.	CUD	CUD	CUD	ble.	ble.	

TABLE 28, Part 1 (*cont.*)

Informant No.	/A/	/Ē/	/I/	/Ou/	/Q/	/O/	/Oi/
74	[ɛɩ] CUD	[ü̈] CUD	*	[äω] CUD	[əü] CUD	[ʔω] CUD	[ɔɩ] CUD
75	[e̦ː]	[iː]	[ʋɩ]	[äü] CUD	[yː]	[o̦ː]	[ɔɩ] RP
76	[ɛɩ] ble.	[ui] RP	*	[aω] CUD+	[əü] CUD	[ʔω] RP+	[ʔ̧ɩ]
77	[e̦ɩ] RP	[iː]	[ʋɩ]	[äω] CUD	[əü] CUD+ble.	[ɔ̈ω]	[əɩ]
78	[ɛɩ] CUD	[ü̈] CUD	[äɩ] CUD+	[äω] RP+	[əü] CUD	[ɔ̈ω] ble.	[ɔɩ] CUD
80	[ɛɩ] CUD	[ü̈] CUD	[äɩ] CUD	[äω] CUD	[əü] CUD	[ʔω] CUD	[ɔɩ] CUD
82	[e̦ɩ] RP	[ui] RP	[äɩ] RP	[aω] RP	[ʉu] ble.	[ʔω] ble.	[ɔɩ] CUD
83	[ɛ̧ɩ] CUD+	*	[äɩ] RP	[aω] CUD+	[ou] RP	[ɒω] CUD+	[ʔ̧ɩ] RP
84	[ɛɩ] CUD	[ü̈] CUD	[äɩ] CUD	[äω] CUD	[əü] CUD	[ɒω] CUD+	[ɔɩ] RP
85	[ɛ̧ɩ] CUD+	[ü̈] CUD	[aɩ] CUD+	[aə] `	[əü] CUD	[ʔω] CUD	[ɔɩ] RP
86	[ɛ̧ɩ] CUD+ble.	[ui] CUD+	[aɩ] RP	[ä̈ω] CUD	[əü] CUD	[ɔ̈ω] ble.	[ʔ̧ɩ] RP
87	[ɛ̧ɩ] CUD+	[ü̈] CUD	[aɩ] CUD+	[äω] CUD	[əü] CUD	[o̦ː]	[ʔ̧ɩ]
88	[ɛɩ] CUD	[əɩ] CUD+	[aɩ] CUD+	[aω] CUD+	[əü] CUD	[ʔω] CUD	[ʔ̧ɩ]
89	[ɛ̧ɩ] CUD+	[ü̈] CUD	[ɒ̈ɩ] CUD+	[äω] CUD	[əü] CUD	[ɒω] CUD+	[ɔɩ] CUD
91	[ɛɩ] CUD	[ui] RP	[äɩ] RP	[äω] CUD	[əü] CUD	[ɔ̈ω] ble.	[əɩ] RP
92	[ɛ̧ɩ] CUD+	[ü̈] CUD	[äɩ] CUD	[äω] CUD	[əü] CUD	[ʔω] CUD	[ɔ̈ɩ]
93	[ɛɩ] CUD	[ü̈] CUD	[aɩ] CUD+	[äω] CUD	[əü] CUD	[ʔω] CUD	[ɒɩ]

TABLE 28, Part 2

Informant No.	/A/	/E/	/I/	/U/	/ʔ/	/O/
1	[a] CUD	[ɛ] ble.	[ɩ] CUD	[ʌ̈] ble.	[ʉ] CUD+	[p̈] CUD+
3	[a] CUD	[e̦] RP	[ɩ] CUD	[ɤ̈] ble.	[ʉ] CUD+	[e̦ː]

TABLE 28, Part 2 (cont.)

Informant No.	/A/	/E/	/I/	/U/	/Q/	/O/
4	[ä]	[ɛ]	[ɪ]	nil	[ɔ]	[ɒ]
	CUD+	CUD	CUD	CUD	CUD	RP
5	[ä]	[ɛ]	[ɪ]	[ÿ]	[ɔ]	[ɒ]
	CUD+	CUD	CUD	ble.	CUD	CUD
7	[a]	[ɛ̣]	[ɪ]	[Ä]	[ʉ]	[ɒ]
	CUD	RP	CUD	ble.	CUD+	RP
8	[a]	[ɛ̣]	[ɪ]	[Ä]	[ʉ]	*
	CUD	RP	CUD	ble.	CUD+	
9	[a]	[ɛ]	[ɪ]	[ÿ]	[ɔ]	[ʔ]
	CUD	ble.	CUD	ble.	CUD	RP+
10	[a]	[ɛ]	[ɪ]	[ÿ]	[ʉ]	[ʔ]
	CUD	CUD	RP	ble.	CUD+	RP+
11	[a]	[ɛ]	[ɪ]	[Ä]	[ɔ]	[ɒ]
	CUD	ble.	RP	ble.	RP	RP
12	[a]	[ɛ̣]	[ɪ]	*	[ɔ]	[Ä]
	CUD	RP	RP			
13	[ä]	[ɛ]	[ɪ]	nil	[ɔ]	[ʔ]
	CUD+	CUD	CUD	CUD	CUD	RP+
14	[a]	[ɛ]	[ɪ]	[Ä]	[ʉ]	[ʔ]
	CUD	ble.	RP	ble.	CUD+	RP+
15	*	[ɛ]	[ɪ]	[Ä]	[ɔ]	[ʔ]
		CUD	RP	ble.	CUD	RP+
16	[æ]	[ɛ̣]	[ɪ]	[ɐ]	[ɔ]	[ɒ]
	RP	RP	RP	RP	RP	RP
18	[ä]	[ɛ]	[ɪ]	[Ä]	[ʉ]	[ɒ]
	CUD+	ble.	RP	ble.	CUD+	CUD
19	[a]	[ɛ̣]	[ɪ]	nil	[ʉ]	[ɒ]
	CUD	RP		CUD	CUD+	CUD
20	[a]	[ɛ̣]	[ɪ]	*	[ɔ]	[ɒ]
	CUD	RP	CUD		CUD	CUD
21	*	[ɛ]	[ɪ]	*	*	[ɒ]
		CUD	CUD			CUD
22	[ä]	[ɛ]	[ɪ]	nil	[ɔ]	[ʔ]
	CUD+	CUD	CUD	CUD	CUD	RP+
23	[a]	[ɛ]	[ɪ]	[Ä]	[ɔ]	[ɒ]
	CUD	CUD	RP	ble.	CUD	CUD
25	[a]	[ɛ]	[ɪ]	[Ä]	[ɔ]	[ɒ]
	CUD	ble.	RP	ble.	RP	RP
26	[ä]	*	[ɪ]	[Ä]	[ɔ]	[ɒ]
	CUD+		CUD	ble.	CUD	RP
28	[æ]	[e]	[ë]	[ɐ]	[ʉ]	[ö]
	RP	RP+	RP+	RP	CUD+	CUD+
29	[æ]	[ɛ]	[ɪ]	[ɐ]	[ɔ]	[ʔ]
	RP	ble.	RP	RP	RP	RP+

TABLE 28, Part 2 (*cont.*)

Informant No.	/A/	/E/	/I/	/U/	/Q/	/O/
30	[a] CUD	[ɛ] RP	[ɪ] CUD	nil CUD	[ɵ] CUD	[ɒ] CUD
31	[ä] CUD+	[ɛ] RP	[ɪ̈]	[ÿ] ble.	[ɵ]	[ɔ]
33	[a] CUD	[ɛ] CUD	[ɪ] CUD	[Λ̈] ble.	[ʉ] CUD+	[ɒ̈] CUD+
34	[ä] CUD+	[ɛ] RP	[ɪ] RP	[ÿ] ble.	[ʉ] CUD+	[ɒ] RP
35	[a] CUD	[ɛ] CUD	[ë] RP+	[ÿ] ble.	[ɵ] CUD	[ɒ] RP
36	[ä] CUD+	[ɛ] RP	[ɪ] CUD	[ÿ] ble.	[ɵ] CUD	[ɒ̈] CUD+
37	[a] CUD	[ɛ] RP	[ɪ] CUD	[Λ̈] ble.	[ɵ] CUD	*
38	[a] CUD	[ɛ] ble.	[ɪ] RP	[ɐ] RP	[ɵ] RP	[ɒ] CUD
39	[ä] CUD+	[ɛ] CUD	[ɪ] CUD	[Λ̈] ble.	[ɵ] CUD	[ɒ] CUD
40	[ä] CUD+	*	[ɪ] RP	[Λ̈] ble.	[ɵ] CUD	[ɒ] CUD
41	[ä] CUD+	[ɛ] RP	[ë] RP+	[Λ̈] ble.	[ɵ] CUD	[ɑ] CUD+
42	[a] CUD	[ɛ] CUD	[ɪ] CUD	[Λ] ble.	[ʉ] CUD+	[ɒ] CUD
43	[a] CUD	[ɛ] RP	[ɪ] CUD	[ɔ̇] ble.	[ʉ] CUD+	[ɒ] CUD
44	[a] CUD	[ɛ] CUD	[ɪ] RP	[ÿ] ble.	[ɵ] CUD	[ɔ̃] CUD+
45	[a] CUD	[ɛ] CUD	[ɪ] CUD	[ÿ] ble.	[ʉ] CUD+	[ɒ̈] CUD+
46	[a] CUD	[ɛ] RP	[ɪ] RP	*	[ɵ] RP	[ɔ] RP+
48	[a] CUD	[ɛ] CUD	[ɪ] CUD	nil CUD	[ɵ] CUD	[ɔ] RP+
49	[ä] CUD+	[ɛ] CUD	[ɪ] RP	[ÿ] ble.	[ɵ] CUD	[ɒ] CUD
50	[ä] CUD+	[ɛ] CUD	[ɪ] RP	[Λ̈] ble.	[ʉ] CUD+	[ɔ̇] RP+
51	[æ] RP	[ɛ] CUD	[ɪ] RP	[ɐ̝] RP	[ɵ] RP	[ɒ] RP
52	[æ] RP	[ɛ] CUD	[ɪ] RP	[ɐ] RP	[ʉ] CUD+	[ɒ̈] CUD+
53	[ä] CUD+	[ɛ] ble.	[ɨ]	[ÿ] ble.	[ʏ]	[ǫ]

TABLE 28, Part 2 (*cont.*)

Informant Non.	/A/	/E/	/I/	/U/	/Q/	/O/
54	[a] CUD	[e] RP+	[ɪ] CUD	[ÿ] ble.	[ʉ] CUD+	[ä]
55	[a] CUD	[ɛ̞] RP	[ɪ̞] CUD	[Ä] ble.	[ɷ] CUD	[ö̞] CUD+
56	[a] CUD	[ɛ] CUD	[ɪ] RP	[Ä] ble.	[ɷ] CUD	[ɔ̞̈] CUD+
57	[a] CUD	[ɛ̞] RP	*	*	[ɷ] RP	[ɒ] RP
60	[æ] RP	[ɛ̞] RP	[ɪ] RP	[ɐ̯] RP	[ʉ] CUD+	*
61	[a] CUD	[ɛ̞] ble.	[ɪ] RP	[ɐ̯] RP	[ʉ] CUD+	*
62	[a] CUD	[ɛ] CUD	[ɪ] RP	[Ä̈] ble.	[ʉ] CUD+	[ɑ] CUD+
63	[a] CUD	[e] RP+	[ɪ̞] CUD	[Ä̈] ble.	[ɥ] CUD+	[ɒ] CUD
64	[a] CUD	[ɛ] CUD	[ɪ̞] CUD	[ÿ] ble.	[ɷ] CUD	[ɑ] CUD+
65	[æ] RP	[ɛ̞] CUD+	[ɪ] RP	[ɐ̯] RP	[ɷ] RP	[ɔ] RP+
66	[a] CUD	*	[ɪ̞] CUD	*	[ɷ] CUD	[ɒ] RP
67	[a] CUD	[ɛ̞] RP	[ɪ̞] CUD	[ÿ] ble.	[ʉ] CUD+	[ä] CUD+
68	[æ] RP	[ɛ̞] RP	[ɪ] RP	[ɐ̯] RP	[ɷ] RP	[ɒ] CUD
69	[ä] CUD+	[ɛ̞] RP	[ɪ̞] CUD	[ÿ̈] ble.	[ɷ] CUD	[ɒ] CUD
71	[a] CUD	[ɛ̞] RP	[ɪ̞] CUD	[ʉ] CUD	[ɷ] CUD	[ɔ̞̈] CUD+
72	[a] CUD	[ɛ] CUD	[ɪ] RP	[Ä] ble.	[ʉ] CUD+	[ɔ] RP+
73	[a] CUD	[ɛ] ble.	[ɪ̞] CUD	nil CUD	[ɷ] CUD	[ɒ] CUD
74	[ä] CUD+	[ɛ] CUD	[ɪ] CUD	[Ä̈] ble.	[ɷ] CUD	[ɔ] RP+
75	[ä] CUD+	[ɛ] ble.	[i]	[ÿ̈]	[ɤ]	[ɔ]
76	[a] CUD	[ɛ̞] RP	[ɪ̞] CUD	[Ä̈] ble.	[ʉ] CUD+	[ɒ] CUD
77	[a] CUD	[ɛ̞] RP	[ɪ] RP	*	[ʉ] CUD+	[ö̞] CUD+
78	[ä] CUD+	[ɛ] CUD	[ɪ̞] CUD	nil CUD	[ɷ] CUD	[ɔ̞̈] CUD+

TABLE 28, Part 2 (cont.)

Informant No.i

No.i	/A/	/E/	/I/	/U/	/Q/	/O/
80	[ä] CUD+	[ɛ] CUD	[ɪ] CUD	[Λ̈] ble.	[ɵ] CUD	[ɒ] CUD
82	[a] CUD	[ɛ̣] RP	[ɩ] RP	[ɐ] RP	[ɵ] RP	[ɔ] RP+
83	[a] CUD	[ɛ̣] RP	[ɪ] CUD	[ɐ̥] RP	[ɵ] CUD	[ä] CUD+
84	[ä] CUD+	[ɛ] CUD	[ɪ] CUD	nil CUD	[ɵ] CUD	[ɒ] CUD
85	[ä] CUD+	[ɛ̣] CUD+	[ɪ] CUD	nil CUD	[ɵ] CUD	*
86	[ä] CUD+	[ɛ] CUD	[ë] RP+	[ɣ̈] ble.	[ʉ] CUD+	[ɐ]
87	[ä] CUD+	[ɛ] CUD	[ɩ] RP	[ÿ] ble.	[ɵ] CUD	[ɑ] CUD+
88	[a] CUD	[ɛ] CUD	[ɪ] CUD	nil CUD	[ɵ] CUD	*
89	[a] CUD	[ɛ] CUD	[ɪ] CUD	nil CUD	[ɵ] CUD	[ɚ] RP+
91	[a] CUD	[ɛ] CUD	[ɪ] CUD	[ɐ] RP	[ɵ] CUD	[ɚ] RP+
92	[a] CUD	[ɛ] CUD	[ɩ] CUD	[ÿ̈] ble.	[ɵ] CUD	[ɒ] CUD
93	[ä] CUD+	[ɛ] CUD	[ɪ] CUD	nil CUD	[ɵ] CUD	[ɒ̈] CUD+

Table 28, Part 3

Informant No.

No.	/AR/		/ER/		/OR/		/ĀR/	
1	[ä:]		[ə:]	RP	[ɒ:]	CUD+	[ɛə]	RP
3	[ä:]		[ə:]	RP	[ɔ:]	RP	[ɛ̣:ə]	RP+
4	[ɑ:]	CUD+	[ə:]	CUD	[ɔ̣:]	CUD	[ɛ̣:]	CUD+
5	[ɑ:]	CUD+	[ə̣:]	CUD	[ɔ̣:]	CUD	[ɛə]	RP
7	[ä:]	CUD	[ə:]	RP	[ɔ:]	CUD	[ɛ̣:]	RP+
8	[ä:]	CUD	[ə̣:]	CUD	[ɔ̣:]	CUD	[ɛ̣ə]	RP+
9	[ɑ:]	CUD+	[ɛ̈:]	CUD+	[ɔ:]	CUD	[ɛ:]	CUD
10	[ɑ:]	CUD+	[ə̣:]	CUD	[ɔ:]	CUD	[ɛ:]	CUD
11	[ɑ:]	RP+	[ə:]	RP	[ɔ:]	RP	[ɛə]	RP
12	[ä:]		[ɤ̈:]	CUD+	[ɔ̈:]	CUD+	[ɛ̣:]	
13	[ɑ:]	CUD+	[ɛ:]	CUD+	[ɔ̣:]	CUD	[ɛ:]	CUD
14	[ä]	CUD	[ə̣:]	CUD	[ɔ̣:]	CUD+	[ɛ:]	CUD
15	[ɑ:]	CUD+	[ə̣:]	CUD+	[ɔ̣:]	CUD	[ɛə]	RP
16	[ä:]	RP	[ə̣:]	CUD+	[ɔ:]	RP	[ɛə]	RP
18	[ä:]	CUD	[ə̣:]	CUD	[ɔ:]	CUD	[ɛə]	RP

TABLE 28, Part 3 (*cont.*)

Informant

No.	/AR/		/ER/		/OR/		/ĀR/	
19	[ä:]	CUD	[ë:]	CUD+	[ʔ:]	CUD+	[çə]	RP
20	[ä:]	CUD	[ə:]	CUD	[ɔ:]	CUD	[ɛ:]	CUD
21	[ɑ:]	CUD+	[ʒ:]	RP+	[ɔ:]	CUD	[çə]	RP
22	*		[ë:]	CUD+	[ʔ:]	CUD	[ɛ:]	CUD
23	[ä:]	CUD	[ə̣:]	CUD+	[ʔ:]	CUD+	[ɛə]	RP
25	[ä:]	RP	[ʒ:]	RP+	[ɔ:]	RP	[ɛ:]	CUD
26	[ɑ:]	CUD+	[ë:]	CUD+	[ɔ̇:]	CUD	[ɛə]	RP
28	[ä:]	RP	[ʔ:]	RP+	[ö:]	CUD+	[ɛə]	RP
29	[ä:]	RP	[ə:]	RP	[ɔ:]	RP	[ɛə]	RP
30	[ä:]	CUD	[ï:]	CUD+	[ɔ:]	CUD+	[ɛə]	RP
31	[ɒ:]		[œ:]		[ǫ:]		[çə]	RP+
33	[ä:]	CUD	[ə:]	RP	[ʔ:]	CUD	[ɛ:]	CUD
34	[ɑ:]	CUD+	[ʔ:]		[ɔ:]	CUD	[çə]	RP
35	[ɑ:]	CUD+	[ʔ:]	RP+	[ǫ:]	CUD+	[çə]	RP
36	[ä:]	CUD	[ə:]	CUD	[ɔ̈:]	CUD+	[ɛə]	RP
37	[ä:]	CUD	[ə̣:]	CUD	[ɔ:]	CUD	[ɛ:]	CUD
38	[ä:]	RP	[ɔ:]	RP	[ʔ:]	CUD+	[ɛə]	RP
39	[ä:]	CUD	[ə:]	RP	[ɔ:]	CUD	[ɛ:]	CUD
40	[ä:]	CUD	[ə:]	CUD	[ɔ:]	CUD	[ɛə]	RP
41	[ä:]	CUD	[ɪ:]		[o:]		[ɛɹ]	
42	[ä:]	CUD	[ʒ:]	RP+	[ɒ:]	CUD+	[ɛə]	RP
43	[ɑ:]	CUD+	[ə:]	CUD	[ɔ:]	CUD	[çə]	RP
44	[ä:]	CUD	[ʒ:]		[ɔ:]	CUD	[ɛ:]	CUD
45	[ä:]	CUD	[ʒ:]	CUD+	[ɒ:]	CUD+	[ɛ:]	CUD
46	*		[ə:]	RP	[ɔ:]	RP	[ɛə]	RP
48	[ɑ:]	CUD+	*		[ɔ:]	CUD	*	
49	[ɑ:]	CUD+	[ə:]	CUD	[ɔ:]	CUD	[ɛ:]	CUD
50	[ɑ:]	CUD+	*		[ɔ:]	CUD	[ɛə]	RP
51	[ä:]	RP	[ʔ:]	RP+	[ɔ:]	RP	[ɛə]	RP
52	[ä:]	CUD	[ə:]	RP	[ɔ̈:]	CUD+	[ɛə]	RP
53	[ä:]		[ər]		[ö:]		[eɚr]	
54	[ä:]	CUD	[ï:]	CUD+	[ɔ:]	CUD	[ɛ:]	CUD
55	[ä:]	CUD	[ʒ:]	CUD+	[ʔ:]	CUD+	[ɛ:]	CUD
56	[ä:]	CUD	[ʔ:]	RP+	[ɔ:]	CUD	[ɛ:]	CUD
57	[ä:]	RP	[ʒ:]	RP+	[ɔ:]	RP	[çə]	RP+
60	[ä:]	RP	[ʒ:]	RP	[ɔ:]	RP	[ɛə]	RP
61	[ɑ:]	RP+	[ʒ̆:]	CUD+	[ɔ:]	RP	[ɛə]	RP
62	[ɑ:]	CUD+	[ə:]	CUD	[ɔ̇:]	CUD	[ɛə]	RP
63	[ä:]	CUD	[ə̣:]	CUD+	[ɒ:]	CUD+	[ɛə]	RP
64	[ä:]	CUD	[ë:]	CUD+	[ʔ:]	CUD+	[ɛə]	RP
65	[ɒ:]	CUD+	*		[ʔ:]	RP	[çə]	RP+
66	[ɑ:]	CUD+	[ə:]	CUD	[ɔ:]	CUD	[ę:]	RP+
67	[ä:]		[ʒ:]	RP+	[ɔ̈:]	CUD+	[çə]	RP+
68	[ä:]	RP	[ʒ:]	RP+	[ʔ:]	RP	[ɛə]	RP+

TABLE 28, Part 3 (cont.)

Informant No.	/AR/		/ER/		/OR/		/ĀR/	
69	[ɑ:]	CUD+	[ə:]	CUD	[ɔ:]	CUD	[ɛ:]	CUD
71	[ɑ:]	CUD+	[ə̰:]	CUD+	[ɔ:]	CUD	[ɛ:]	CUD
72	[ɑ:]	RP+	[ɚ:]	RP+	[ɔ:]	RP	[ɛə]	RP
73	[ä:]	CUD	[ə:]	CUD	[ɔ̇:]	CUD	[ɛ:]	CUD
74	[ɑ:]	CUD+	[ə̇:]	CUD	[ɔ̇:]	CUD	[ɛə]	RP
75	[äɪ]		*		[ǫɪ]		[ɕəɪ]	
76	[ä:]	CUD	[ə̰:]	CUD+	[ɔ̃:]	CUD+	[ɕə]	RP+
77	[ä:]		[ø:]		[ɔ:]	CUD	[ɛɐ]	RP+
78	[ɑ:]	CUD+	[ə:]	CUD+	[ɔ:]	CUD	[ɛʔə]	ble.
80	[ɑ:]	CUD+	[ə̇:]	CUD	[ǫ:]	CUD+	[ɕə]	RP+
82	[ä:]	RP	[ɚ:]	RP+	[ɔ:]	RP	[ɕə]	RP
83	[ä:]	CUD	[ɚ:]	RP+	[ɚ̇:]	CUD+	[ɛ:]	CUD
84	[ä:]	CUD	[ə̇:]	CUD	[ǫ:]	CUD+	[ɛə]	RP
85	*		[ə̇:]	CUD	[ɔ:]	CUD	[ɛə]	RP
86	[ä:]		*		[ɔ:]	CUD	*	
87	[ä:]		[ə̰:]	CUD+	[ə:]	CUD	[ɛ:]	CUD
88	[ä:]	CUD	[ə̰:]	CUD	[ɔ̇:]	CUD	[ɛ:]	CUD
89	[ɑ:]	CUD+	[ɔ̇:]	CUD+	[ɔ̇:]	CUD	[ɛ:]	CUD
91	[ä:]	CUD	[ə̰:]	CUD+	[ǫ̇:]	CUD+	[ɛə]	RP
92	[ä:]	CUD	[ə̰:]	CUD	[ɔ:]	CUD	[ɛ:]	CUD
93	[ä̈:]	CUD	[ə̰:]	CUD+	[ɔ̈:]	CUD+	[ɛ:]	CUD

Notes on Table 28

Informant No.

3   /Ē/—the pronunciation [ui] occurs in *trees, three, real* and *heel*, but *beat* and *bead* have a pure vowel close to [i:]. RP.

/Ou/—two pronunciations are found, [äɔ] and [äɔ]. ble. The informant has a slight Welsh lilt.

8   /O/—two pronunciations are found, [ɔ] and [ɒ]. ble.

12   /Ā/ and /ĀR/ have the same realisation, [ɛ:]. Both unassignable.

/Ī/ and /Oi/ have the same realisation, [ɐɪ]. Both unassignable.

/ER/ (= [ɤ:]) is the long equivalent of /U/ (= [ɤ̈]). Both unassignable.

This informant has a distinctive Tyneside accent, with a phonological system very different from either RP or CUD.

15   /Ē/—usually pronounced /ui][, but *bead* has [ɥi]. RP.

/Ī/—usually pronounced [äɪ], but *vice* has [äɪ]. CUD.

/A/—both [a] and [ä] occur with equal frequency. CUD+.

20 /U/—see note on this informant in Table 27 above. For the reasons given there we take this to be an influence of the prestige dialect and assume that /U/ is missing. CUD.

21 /A/—both [a] and [ä] occur with equal frequency. CUD+.

/U/ and /Q/ have the same realisation [ÿ], which we take to be the relaxed variety of /Q/ that is found with other informants. This is the only case in the sample of /U/ and /Q/ falling together in a sound other than [ɷ] or [ʉ]. CUD in both cases.

22 /AR/—both [ɑ:] and [ɒ:] occur with equal frequency. CUD+.

26 /Ī/—normally pronounced [äɪ], but *vice* has [ɐɪ] and *wide* has [ɒ̈ɪ]. RP.

/Q/—the realisation [ɷu] is very common, but *zoo* and *two* have [əü]. ble.

/E/—both [ę] and [ɛ] occur with equal frequency. ble.

28 This informant has an unusually high number of unassignable features. Especially noteworthy are the pure vowel realisations of /Ē/ and /Q̄/; possibly these might be attributable to the influence of the informant's Scottish husband.

31 The informant has a distinctive Tyneside accent with some points of contact with RP.

34 This informant has an unusually high number of unassignable features. This might reflect his birth and upbringing on Teesside, although both his parents were Staffordshire people.

37 /O/—the realisation [ɒ] occurs in *doll*, *job* and *pot*; [ɒ̣] occurs in *pod* and *one*. ble.

38 Although RP has a clear majority in this informant's speech, there are sufficient CUD realisations to suggest that this RP accent may not be wholly natural. CUD vowels occur in *wide*, *boat* and *butter*, even though generally these vowels have RP realisations.

39 /Ē/—both [ui] and [ʯi] occur with equal frequency. ble.

/Ī/—both [äɪ] and [ɑ̈ɪ] occur with equal frequency. ble.

40 /Ē/—normally pronounced [ʯi], but *beat* and *three* have [ui]. CUD.

/E/—normally pronounced [ɛ], but *seven* and *ten* have [ę]. CUD.

41 /Q̄/—normally pronounced [əü], but *boot* and *two* have [ɷu]. CUD.

This informant has a noticeable Northern accent, particularly clear in the post-vocalic /R/.

44 /Ī/—both [ɑ̈ɪ] and [äɪ] occur with equal frequency. ble.

46 /Ō/—both [əʊ] and [ʔʊ] occur with equal frequency. ble.

/U/—normally pronounced [ɐ], but *butter* and *one* have [ʌ̈]. ble.

/AR/—pronounced [aː], a mysterious sound for an informant with such a high proportion of RP sounds.

48 /ER/ and /ĀR/ both realised [ɛː]. /ER/ is CUD+; /ĀR/ is CUD.

50 /Ī/—both [äɪ] and [äɪ] occur with equal frequency. ble.

/ER/—both [əː] and [ə̣ː] occur with equal frequency. ble.

51 /Ou/—both [äʊ] and [äʊ] occur with equal frequency. ble.

53 This informant has a clear Scots accent.

54 /Ī/—both [aɪ] and [ọ̈ɪ] occur with equal frequency. ble.

57 /I/—both [ɪ] and [ɪ̣] occur with equal frequency. ble.

/U/—both [ɐ̣] and [ɏ̈] occur with equal frequency. ble.

60 /O/—both [ɒ̣] and [ɒ] occur with equal frequency. ble.

61 /O/—both [ɒ̇] and [ɒ] occur with equal frequency. ble.

64 /Ī/—both [äɪ̇] and [äɪ] occur with equal frequency. ble.

65 [Ī]—normally pronounced [äɪ], but *wide* has [ɒɪ]. ble.

/ER/—realised [ɯː]. The assignment of this vowel is highly tentative. It occurs in the speech of no other informant. CUD+.

The speech of this informant is peculiar. It is strange to find as many as three CUD+ features in a predominantly RP type of speech. Moreover, the pronunciation of many words appeared to be definitely forced.

66 /E/—both [ɛ̣] and [ɛ] occur with equal frequency. ble.

/U/—both [ɐ] and [ʌ̈] occur with equal frequency. ble.

71 /U/ and /Q/ are very similar: /U/ is pronounced [ʉ] and /Q/ = [ʊ]. There may be no genuine phonemic contrast here. CUD in both cases.

74 /Ī/—both [äɪ] and [ɑɪ] occur with equal frequency. CUD+.

75 /ER/—both [əɹ] and [ɛ̣ɹ] occur with equal frequency. Unassignable.

This informant has a clear Scots accent.

76 /Ī/—both [äɪ] and [äɪ] occur with equal frequency. ble.

77 [U]—pronounced [ä]. The same vowel occurs in *dull*, *bud* and *rubber*, as expected, but also in *dance*. RP+.

This informant has a clear Welsh accent, with the typical intonation.

83 /Ē/—both [ui] and [ÿi] occur with equal frequency. ble.

85 /O/—both [ɑ] and [ɔ̣] occur with equal frequency. CUD+.

/AR/—both [ä:] and [ä:] occur with equal frequency. CUD.

86   /ER/ and /ĀR/ are both realised [ə̣ː]. /ER/ is CUD;
       /ĀR/ is unassignable.
       This informant has traces of a Liverpool accent.
88   /O/—both [ɒ̣] and [ɒ] occur with equal frequency. ble.

TABLE 29

This table summarises the assignments of features given in Tables 27
and 28. This information is used in setting up the informant classes
in Chapter V.

Informant No.	RP+	RP	blend	CUD	CUD+	Unassignable
1	0	7	2	10	3	1
3	1	11	3	4	1	3
4	0	2	1	15	5	0
5	1	3	1	14	4	0
7	1	7	4	9	2	0
8	1	5	3	12	2	0
9	1	0	3	15	3	1
10	1	4	2	12	4	0
11	2	11	5	5	0	0
12	0	4	0	4	2	13
13	1	2	0	15	4	1
14	2	3	3	12	3	0
15	1	7	1	10	4	0
16	1	17	1	2	2	0
18	1	8	2	10	2	0
19	1	3	0	13	5	1
20	0	3	2	14	4	0
21	1	5	3	12	2	0
22	1	1	2	13	6	0
23	1	6	1	12	3	0
25	1	10	4	8	0	0
26	0	6	5	7	5	0
28	3	14	0	1	3	2
29	1	15	3	3	1	0
30	0	3	0	16	3	1
31	2	6	1	5	1	8
33	1	5	1	12	3	1
34	1	5	2	7	5	3
35	2	5	3	10	3	0
36	0	4	2	12	4	1
37	0	5	3	13	2	0
38	1	14	2	5	1	0
39	0	3	4	14	2	0
40	0	4	2	15	2	0
41	1	5	2	9	2	4
42	2	4	2	11	4	0

TABLE 29 (*cont.*)

Informant No.	RP+	RP	blend	CUD	CUD+	Unassignable
43	0	5	2	13	3	0
44	0	3	5	13	1	1
45	0	3	2	14	4	0
46	1	15	2	4	0	1
48	1	1	1	13	7	0
49	0	3	3	13	3	1
50	1	6	6	6	4	0
51	2	14	2	5	0	0
52	0	10	0	9	4	0
53	0	4	2	3	1	13
54	2	4	2	10	4	1
55	0	5	2	11	4	1
56	2	3	3	12	2	1
57	3	11	3	5	0	1
60	2	12	5	4	0	0
61	1	11	5	4	2	0
62	0	8	2	9	3	1
63	1	7	2	10	3	0
64	0	3	3	13	4	0
65	3	13	3	1	3	0
66	2	4	2	13	2	0
67	4	4	2	8	3	2
68	5	12	1	4	1	0
69	0	4	3	12	4	0
71	0	2	1	16	4	0
72	3	9	2	8	1	0
73	0	0	5	17	0	1
74	1	5	1	13	3	0
75	0	5	1	2	1	14
76	2	5	4	7	4	1
77	2	9	1	3	3	5
78	1	0	2	16	4	0
80	1	2	2	15	3	0
82	2	16	2	3	0	0
83	2	6	2	8	5	0
84	0	3	0	17	3	0
85	0	2	0	15	5	1
86	1	4	3	8	4	3
87	0	1	2	12	5	3
88	0	2	1	16	3	1
89	1	1	0	16	5	0
91	1	7	2	11	2	0
92	0	1	1	19	1	1
93	0	1	0	14	7	1

Appendix III

The following tables show how the twenty-three features of pronunciation are distributed among the various classes of informants. In the tables the features are numbered in the same way as in Table 16, page 55; and the informant classes are as given on page 59ff. The meaning of the symbols is as follows:

C indicates a feature marked as CUD or CUD+;
R indicates a feature marked as RP or RP+;
B indicates a feature marked as a blend;
I indicates a feature not assigned to any of the other categories.

The actual phonetic realisations are given in the lists of Appendix II.

The summary table, Table 31 on page 124, indicates which type of feature is dominant in each of the five classes. A plain entry in this table indicates a majority of at least 50%; two symbols separated by an oblique stroke mean that two types of feature are present in equal numbers; a symbol in brackets shows a majority of less than 50%.

TABLE 30

Informant No.	1	2	3	4	5	6	7	8	9	10	11	12	13	14	15	16	17	18	19	20	21	22	23
Class A																							
93	C	C	C	B	R	C	C	C	C	C	C	C	I	C	C	C	C	C	C	C	C	C	C
89	C	R	C	C	C	C	C	C	C	C	C	C	C	C	C	C	C	C	R	C	C	C	C
48	C	C	C	B	C	C	C	C	C	C	C	C	R	C	C	C	C	R	C	C	C	C	C
85	C	C	C	B	C	C	C	C	I	C	C	R	C	C	C	C	C	C	C	C	C	C	R
4	C	C	B	C	C	R	C	C	C	C	C	C	C	C	C	C	C	C	R	C	C	C	C
78	C	C	C	B	C	C	C	C	R	C	B	C	C	C	C	C	C	C	C	C	C	C	B
71	C	C	C	B	C	C	C	C	C	C	C	R	C	R	C	C	C	C	C	C	C	C	C
84	C	R	C	C	C	C	C	C	C	C	C	C	R	C	C	C	C	C	C	C	C	C	R
92	C	C	C	R	C	C	C	C	C	C	C	C	C	I	C	C	C	B	C	C	C	C	C

TABLE 30 (cont.)

Informant No.	1	2	3	4	5	6	7	8	9	10	11	12	13	14	15	16	17	18	19	20	21	22	23
22	B	C	C	C	B	C	C	C	C	C	C	B	R	C	C	C	C	C	R	C	C	C	C
13	C	C	C	C	R	C	C	R	C	C	C	C	I	C	C	C	C	C	R	C	C	C	C
88	C	R	C	C	R	C	C	C	C	C	C	C	I	C	C	C	C	C	B	C	C	C	C
30	C	C	C	C	R	C	C	C	C	C	C	C	I	C	R	C	C	C	C	C	C	C	R
19	C	C	C	C	R	C	C	C	C	C	C	C	R	C	R	C	R	C	C	C	C	C	R
20	C	C	C	B	R	R	C	C	C	C	C	C	B	C	C	R	C	C	C	C	C	C	C
5	C	C	C	R	R	C	C	C	C	C	C	C	R	C	C	C	B	C	C	C	C	C	C
80	C	R	C	B	R	C	C	C	C	C	C	C	C	C	C	B	C	C	C	C	C	C	R
9	C	C	C	B	C	C	C	C	C	C	C	C	I	C	B	C	B	C	R	C	C	C	C
87	C	C	C	B	C	C	C	C	C	C	C	I	I	C	C	R	B	C	C	I	C	C	C
64	C	C	C	B	C	C	C	R	B	C	C	C	R	C	C	C	B	C	C	C	C	C	R
45	C	C	C	R	C	R	C	R	C	C	C	C	B	C	C	C	B	C	C	C	C	C	C
40	C	C	C	R	C	C	C	C	C	C	C	B	R	C	C	R	B	C	C	C	C	C	C
73	C	C	C	B	C	C	B	C	C	C	B	B	I	C	B	C	C	C	C	C	C	C	C
36	C	R	C	B	C	R	C	C	C	C	C	C	I	C	R	C	B	C	C	C	C	C	R
69	C	C	B	R	R	R	B	C	C	C	C	C	C	R	C	B	C	C	C	C	C	C	C
33	C	C	C	R	C	C	C	R	R	R	R	C	I	C	C	C	B	C	C	C	R	C	C
10	C	R	C	B	C	C	C	C	C	C	R	C	R	C	C	R	B	C	R	C	C	C	C
49	C	I	C	B	C	R	C	C	C	B	C	R	C	R	C	R	B	C	C	C	C	C	C
43	C	C	C	R	C	R	C	R	C	C	C	B	C	C	R	B	C	C	C	C	C	C	R
74	C	R	C	R	R	R	C	C	C	C	C	C	C	C	C	B	C	R	C	C	C	C	R
39	C	C	C	B	R	C	C	B	B	C	C	C	C	C	C	C	B	C	C	C	R	C	C

Class B

Informant No.	1	2	3	4	5	6	7	8	9	10	11	12	13	14	15	16	17	18	19	20	21	22	23
55	C	C	C	R	R	R	C	C	R	C	C	B	I	C	R	C	B	C	C	C	C	C	C
14	B	C	C	R	C	R	C	C	C	C	C	R	C	C	B	R	B	C	R	C	C	C	C
42	C	C	C	R	C	R	C	C	R	C	C	B	R	C	C	C	B	C	C	C	B	C	R
23	C	C	C	R	R	R	C	C	R	C	C	R	C	C	C	R	B	C	C	C	C	C	R
37	C	C	C	R	C	R	B	R	R	C	C	C	C	C	R	C	B	C	B	C	C	C	C
66	C	C	C	R	C	C	R	C	R	C	C	R	C	C	B	C	B	C	R	C	C	C	B
54	C	R	C	R	C	R	C	C	B	C	C	R	R	C	R	C	B	C	I	C	C	C	C
15	C	C	R	R	R	R	C	C	C	C	C	C	C	C	R	B	C	R	C	C	C	C	R
56	C	R	C	B	C	C	C	R	R	C	B	C	I	C	C	R	B	C	C	C	R	C	C
8	C	C	C	R	C	R	C	C	R	R	B	C	C	C	R	C	B	C	B	C	C	C	R
21	B	C	C	C	R	R	B	C	C	R	R	B	C	C	C	C	C	C	C	C	R	C	R
44	C	I	C	B	C	C	C	R	B	R	B	B	C	C	C	R	B	C	C	C	I	C	C
83	C	C	C	B	R	R	C	B	R	C	R	C	R	C	R	C	R	C	C	C	R	C	C
52	C	C	C	R	C	R	C	C	R	C	C	R	R	R	C	R	R	C	C	C	R	C	R
1	C	R	C	R	R	C	C	C	C	R	C	C	C	C	B	C	B	C	C	I	R	C	R
35	C	C	C	R	C	R	C	C	C	C	B	B	R	C	C	R	C	R	C	R	C	C	R
63	C	C	C	B	R	R	R	R	C	C	R	C	C	R	C	B	C	C	C	C	C	C	R
91	C	C	B	R	C	R	C	R	R	C	C	B	R	C	C	C	R	C	R	C	C	C	R
26	C	R	C	B	R	C	C	R	R	C	B	B	C	C	C	B	C	B	C	R	C	C	R
34	C	C	C	B	R	R	C	C	C	C	I	C	I	C	R	R	B	C	R	C	I	C	R
86	C	R	C	R	C	C	C	B	C	R	C	B	R	C	C	R	B	C	I	I	C	C	I
62	C	C	C	R	R	R	C	R	R	R	C	B	I	C	C	R	B	C	C	C	C	C	R
18	B	C	C	R	R	R	C	C	R	C	R	R	R	C	B	R	B	C	C	C	C	C	R

TABLE 30 (*cont.*)

Informant No.										Feature Numbers												
	1	2	3	4	5	6	7	8	9	10	11	12	13	14	15	16	17	18	19	20	21	22	23

Class C

7	C	R	C	B	C	R	C	R	C	C	B	B	R	C	R	C	B	C	R	C	R	C	R
25	C	C	C	R	C	R	C	R	R	R	B	C	B	C	B	R	B	R	R	R	R	R	C
41	B	R	C	B	I	R	C	R	C	C	C	C	C	C	R	R	B	C	C	C	I	I	I
50	C	C	R	R	C	R	C	B	C	C	B	B	R	C	C	R	B	C	R	C	B	C	R
67	C	R	C	B	C	R	C	R	C	C	C	R	I	C	R	C	B	C	C	I	R	C	R
76	C	R	B	R	C	R	B	R	C	C	C	R	I	C	R	C	B	C	C	C	C	C	R
77	I	R	R	R	R	R	R	I	C	C	C	B	I	C	R	R	R	C	C	I	I	C	R

Class D

38	B	R	R	R	R	R	C	C	R	R	B	R	R	C	B	R	R	R	C	R	R	C	R
57	B	C	C	R	C	R	R	R	R	C	I	R	R	C	R	B	B	R	R	R	R	R	R
60	B	C	C	R	R	R	B	R	R	C	B	R	C	R	R	R	R	B	B	R	R	R	R
11	B	C	C	R	R	R	B	R	C	R	B	C	R	C	B	R	B	R	R	R	R	R	R
72	C	R	C	R	C	R	C	R	R	R	B	C	C	C	R	B	C	R	R	R	R	R	R
3	C	R	R	R	R	R	C	R	R	B	R	B	I	C	R	C	B	C	I	I	R	R	R
61	C	C	C	R	R	R	B	R	R	R	B	B	R	C	B	R	R	C	B	R	C	R	R

Class E

82	C	R	R	R	R	R	R	R	R	R	B	B	C	C	R	R	R	R	R	R	R	R	R
16	R	C	R	R	B	R	C	R	R	C	C	R	R	R	R	R	R	R	R	R	C	R	R
68	B	R	C	R	R	R	R	R	C	B	R	R	R	R	R	R	R	C	R	R	R	R	R
28	R	R	C	R	R	R	R	I	R	R	I	R	R	R	R	R	R	C	C	R	R	C	R
65	B	R	B	R	R	C	R	R	B	R	R	R	R	R	C	R	R	R	R	C	C	R	R
51	R	R	C	R	C	R	C	R	C	B	B	R	R	R	C	R	R	R	R	R	R	R	R
46	R	R	C	R	R	R	R	R	C	R	B	C	C	R	R	B	R	R	I	R	R	R	R
29	R	C	C	R	R	R	B	R	R	C	B	R	C	R	B	R	R	R	R	R	R	R	R

TABLE 31

Feature	Class A	Class B	Class C	Class D	Class E
1	C	C	C	B	R
2	C	C	R	C	R
3	C	C	C	C	C
4	B	R	R	R	R
5	C	C/R	C	R	R
6	C	R	R	R	R
7	C	C	C	(C)	R
8	C	C	R	R	R
9	C	R	(R)	R	R
10	C	C	C	R	C
11	C	C	C	B	B
12	C	(B)	(B)	(R)	R
13	(R)	(C)	(I)	R	R
14	C	C	C	C	R
15	C	(C)	R	(B/R)	R
16	C	C	R	R	R
17	C/B	B	B	(B/R)	R
18	C	C	C	(C/R)	R
19	C	C	C	(R)	R
20	C	C	C	R	R
21	C	C	(R)	R	R
22	C	C	C	R	R
23	C	R	R	R	R

Appendix IV

This appendix gives the detailed results of applying the χ^2 test to the survey material; a summary of the results will be found in Table 22 on page 72. For convenience, Table 21, which is an extract from a χ^2 table, is repeated here.

TABLE 21
(Value of χ^2)

Degree of freedom	Percentage level					
	10%	5%	2·5%	1%	0·5%	0·1%
2	4·61	5·99	7·38	9·21	10·60	13·81
4	7·78	9·49	11·14	13·28	14·86	18·47

The observed and expected data are combined in one chart: in each cell, observed data in the top left-hand corner and expected data in the bottom right.

Index to χ^2 results

Results of χ^2 tests

1. *Linguistic class and sex*

	Class A		Class B		Classes C, D and E		
Male	27	16·8	7	12·4	7	11·8	(41)
Female	4	14·2	16	10·6	15	10·2	(35)
	(31)		(23)		(22)		(76)

$\chi^2 = 22\cdot85$ with two degrees of freedom. From Table 21 we conclude that there is a relationship between Linguistic Class and Sex, significant at the $0\cdot1\%$ level.

2. *Linguistic Class and Age*

	Class A		Class B		Classes C, D and E		
Young	12	11·9	9	8·7	8	8·4	(29)
Middle-Aged	14	11·3	3	8·5	11	8·2	(28)
Elderly	5	7·8	11	5·8	3	5·4	(19)
	(31)		(23)		(22)		(76)

$\chi^2 = 12\cdot64$ with four degrees of freedom. From Table 21 we conclude that there is a relationship between Linguistic Class and Age, significant at the $2\cdot5\%$ level.

3. *Linguistic Class and Income Group*

	Class A		Class B		Classes C, D and E		
Less than £1000	18		13		5		(36)
		15·0		10·5		10·5	
More than £1000	12		8		16		(36)
		15·0		10·5		10·5	
	(30)		(21)		(21)		(72)

$\chi^2 = 8\cdot16$ with two degrees of freedom. From Table 21 we conclude that there is a relationship between Linguistic Class and Income Group, significant at the $2\cdot5\%$ level.

Note: in this case the row and column totals are smaller, because four informants did not know their income.

4. *Linguistic Class and Social Class*

	Class A		Class B		Classes C, D and E		
Intermediate and Skilled Non-manual	1		7		17		(25)
		10·2		7·6		7·2	
Skilled Manual and Semi-skilled Non-manual	19		12		4		(35)
		14·3		10·6		10·1	
Semi-skilled Manual	11		4		1		(16)
		6·5		4·8		4·7	
	(31)		(23)		(22)		(76)

$\chi^2 = 33\cdot25$ with four degrees of freedom. From Table 21 we conclude that there is a relationship between Linguistic Class and Social Class, significant at the $0\cdot1\%$ level.

5. *Linguistic Class and Place of Birth*

	Class A		Class B		Classes C, D and E		
Born in Cannock	22	17·5	12	13·0	9	12·5	(43)
Born up to fourteen miles away	9	9·0	8	6·7	5	6·3	(22)
Born more than fourteen miles away	0	4·5	3	3·3	8	3·2	(11)
	(31)		(23)		(22)		(76)

$\chi^2 = 14\cdot47$ with four degrees of freedom. From Table 21 we conclude that there is a relationship between Linguistic Class and Place of Birth, significant at the 1% level.

6. *Linguistic Class and Time lived in Cannock*

	Class A		Class B		Classes C, D and E		
Whole of life	17	13·5	9	9·4	5	8·1	(31)
50%–99%	10	11·8	9	8·8	10	8·4	(29)
Less than 50%	4	5·7	5	4·8	7	5·5	(16)
	(31)		(23)		(22)		(76)

$\chi^2 = 3\cdot66$ with four degrees of freedom. From Table 21 we conclude that there is no significant relationship between Linguistic Class and Time lived in Cannock.

7. *Linguistic Class and Length of Schooling*

	Class A		Class B		Classes C, D and E		
Minimum schooling	31		18		14		(63)
		25·7		19·1		18·2	
Extra years	0		5		8		(13)
		5·3		3·9		3·8	
		(31)		(23)		(22)	(76)

$\chi^2 = 12\cdot37$ with two degrees of freedom. From Table 21 we conclude that there is a relationship between Linguistic Class and Length of Schooling, significant at the 0·5% level.

8. *Sex and Age*

	Young		Middle-aged		Elderly		
Male	15		18		8		(41)
		15·6		15·1		10·3	
Female	14		10		11		(35)
		13·4		12·9		8·7	
	(29)		(28)		(19)		(76)

$\chi^2 = 2\cdot42$ with two degrees of freedom. From Table 21 we conclude that there is no significant relationship between Sex and Age.

9. *Sex and Social Class*

	Male		Female		
Intermediate and Skilled Non-manual	8		17		(25)
		13·5		11·5	
Skilled Manual and Semi-skilled Non-manual	23		12		(35)
		18·9		16·1	
Semi-skilled Manual	10		6		(16)
		8·6		7·4	
	(41)		(35)		(76)

$\chi^2 = 7\cdot29$ with two degrees of freedom. From Table 21 we conclude that there is a relationship between Sex and Social Class, significant at the 5% level.

10. *Sex and Place of Birth*

	Male		Female		
Born in Cannock	27		16		(43)
		23·2		19·8	
Born up to fourteen miles away	9		13		(22)
		11·8		10·2	
Born more than fourteen miles away	5		6		(11)
		6·0		5·0	
		(41)		(35)	(76)

$\chi^2 = 3·15$ with two degrees of freedom. From Table 21 we conclude that there is no significant relationship between Sex and Place of Birth.

11. *Sex and Time lived in Cannock*

	Male		Female		
Whole of Life	21		10		(31)
		16·7		14·3	
50%–99%	13		16		(29)
		15·6		13·4	
Less than 50%	7		9		(16)
		8·7		7·3	
		(41)		(35)	(76)

$\chi^2 = 4·06$ with two degrees of freedom. From Table 21 we conclude that there is no significant relationship between Sex and Time lived in Cannock.

12. *Age and Income Group*

	Less than £1000		More than £1000		
Young	12		16		(28)
		14·0		14·0	
Middle-Aged	9		18		(27)
		13·5		13·5	
Elderly	15		2		(17)
		8·5		8·5	
		(36)		(36)	(72)

$\chi^2 = 18\cdot66$ with two degrees of freedom. From Table 21 we conclude that there is a relationship between Age and Income Group, significant at the $0\cdot1\%$ level.

Note: in this case the row and column totals are smaller, because four informants did not know their income.

13. *Age and Social Class*

	Young		Middle-Aged		Elderly		
Intermediate and Skilled Non-manual	15		7		3		(25)
		9·5		9·2		6·3	
Skilled Manual and Semi-skilled Non-manual	7		14		14		(35)
		13·4		12·9		8·7	
Semi-skilled Manual	7		7		2		(16)
		6·1		5·9		4·0	
		(29)		(28)		(19)	(76)

$\chi^2 = 13\cdot11$ with four degrees of freedom. From Table 21 we conclude that there is a relationship between Age and Social Class, significant at the $2\cdot5\%$ level.

14. *Age and Place of Birth*

	Young	Middle-Aged	Elderly	
Born in Cannock	18	14	11	(43)
	16·4	15·8	10·8	
Born up to fourteen miles away	9	7	6	(22)
	8·4	8·1	5·5	
Born more than fourteen miles away	2	7	2	(11)
	4·2	4·1	2·7	
	(29)	(28)	(19)	(76)

$\chi^2 = 3·99$ with four degrees of freedom. From Table 21 we conclude that there is no significant relationship between Age and Place of Birth.

15. *Age and Time lived in Cannock*

	Young	Middle-Aged	Elderly	
Whole of Life	14	10	7	(31)
	11·8	11·4	7·8	
50%–99%	5	15	9	(29)
	11·1	10·7	7·2	
Less than 50%	10	3	3	(16)
	6·1	5·9	4·0	
	(29)	(28)	(19)	(76)

$\chi^2 = 10·36$ with four degrees of freedom. From Table 21 we conclude that there is a relationship between Age and Time lived in Cannock, significant at the 5% level.

16. *Age and Length of Schooling*

	Young	Middle-Aged	Elderly	
Minimum Schooling	23 24·0	26 23·2	14 15·8	(63)
Extra Years	6 5·0	2 4·8	5 3·2	(13)
	(29)	(28)	(19)	(76)

$\chi^2 = 3\cdot47$ with two degrees of freedom. From Table 21 we conclude that there is no significant relationship between Age and Length of Schooling.

17. *Income Group and Social Class*

	Less than £1000	More than £1000	
Intermediate and Skilled Non-manual	8 12·5	17 12·5	(25)
Skilled Manual and Semi-skilled Non-manual	18 16·5	15 16·5	(33)
Semi-skilled Manual	10 7·0	4 7·0	(14)
	(36)	(36)	(72)

$\chi^2 = 6\cdot10$ with two degrees of freedom. From Table 21 we conclude that there is a relationship between Income Group and Social Class, significant at the 5% level.

Note: in this case the row and column totals are smaller, because four informants did not know their income.

18. *Income Group and Place of Birth*

	Less than £1000		More than £1000		
Born in Cannock	18		23		(41)
		20·5		20·5	
Born up to fourteen miles away	11		9		(20)
		10·0		10·0	
Born more than fourteen miles away	7		4		(11)
		5·5		5·5	
		(36)		(36)	(72)

$\chi^2 = 1·62$ with two degrees of freedom. From Table 21 we conclude that there is no significant relationship between Income Group and Place of Birth.

Note: in this case the row and column totals are smaller, because four informants did not know their income.

19. *Income Group and Time lived in Cannock*

	Less than £1000		More than £1000		
Whole of Life	15		14		(29)
		14·5		14·5	
50%–99%	14		14		(28)
		14·0		14·0	
Less than 50%	7		8		(15)
		7·5		7·5	
		(36)		(36)	(72)

$\chi^2 = 0·10$ with two degrees of freedom. From Table 21 we conclude that there is no significant realtionship between Income Group and Time lived in Cannock.

Note: in this case the row and column totals are smaller, because four informants did not know their income.

20. *Social Class and Place of Birth*

	Born in Cannock	Born up to fourteen miles away	Born more than fourteen miles away	
Intermediate and Skilled Non-manual	11 14·1	7 7·2	7 3·7	(25)
Skilled Manual and Semi-skilled Non-manual	26 19·8	7 10·1	2 5·1	(35)
Semi-skilled Manual	6 9·1	8 4·7	2 2·8	(16)
	(43)	(22)	(11)	(76)

$\chi^2 = 12\cdot01$ with four degrees of freedom. From Table 21 we conclude that there is a relationship between Social Class and Place of Birth, significant at the 2·5% level.

21. *Social Class and Time lived in Cannock*

	Whole of Life	50%–99%	Less than 50%	
Intermediate and Skilled Non-manual	7 10·2	9 9·5	9 5·3	(25)
Skilled Manual and Semi-skilled Non-manual	19 14·3	14 13·4	2 7·3	(35)
Semi-skilled Manual	5 6·5	6 6·1	5 3·4	(16)
	(31)	(29)	(16)	(76)

$\chi^2 = 10\cdot13$ with four degrees of freedom. From Table 21 we conclude that there is a relationship between Social Class and Time lived in Cannock, significant at the 5% level.

22. *Social Class and Length of Schooling*

	Minimum Schooling		Extra Years		
Intermediate and Skilled Non-manual	14	20·7	11	4·3	(25)
Skilled Manual and Semi-skilled Non-manual	33	29·0	2	6·0	(35)
Semi-skilled Manual	16	13·3	0	2·7	(16)
	(63)		(13)		(76)

$\chi^2 = 19\cdot08$ with two degrees of freedom. From Table 21 we conclude that there is a relationship between Social Class and Length of Schooling, significant at the $0\cdot1\%$ level.

23. *Place of Birth and Time lived in Cannock*

	Whole of Life		50%–99%		Less than 50%			
Born in Cannock	31	31·0	12	7·7	0	4·3	(12)	(43)
Born up to fourteen miles away			13	14·2	9	7·8	(22)	
Born more than fourteen miles away			4	7·1	7	3·9	(11)	
	(31)		(29)		(16)		(45)	(76)

$\chi^2 = 10\cdot79$ with two degrees of freedom. From Table 21 we conclude that there is a relationship between Place of Birth and Time lived in Cannock, significant at the $0\cdot5\%$ level.

Note: If one has lived the whole of one's life in Cannock, then one must have been born there. This excludes the thirty-one informants concerned from the significance test.

24. *Place of Birth and Length of Schooling*

	Minimum Schooling		Extra Years		
Born in Cannock	41	35·6	2	7·4	(43)
Born up to fourteen miles away	15	18·2	7	3·8	(22)
Born more than fourteen miles away	7	9·2	4	1·8	(11)
	(63)		(13)		(76)

$\chi^2 = 11·23$ with two degrees of freedom. From Table 21 we conclude that there is a relationship between Place of Birth and Length of Schooling, significant at the 0·5% level.

25. *Time lived in Cannock and Length of Schooling*

	Minimum Schooling		Extra Years		
Whole of Life	29	25·7	2	5·3	(31)
50%–99%	24	24·0	5	5·0	(29)
Less than 50%	10	13·3	6	2·7	(16)
	(63)		(13)		(76)

$\chi^2 = 7·32$ with two degrees of freedom. From Table 21 we conclude that there is a relationship between Time lived in Cannock and Length of Schooling, significant at the 5% level.

Bibliography

Allen, W. S., *Vox Latina*, Cambridge University Press, 1965.

Bloomfield, L., *Language*, George Allen & Unwin Ltd., London 1933.

Bowyer, R. A., *A Study of Social Accents in a South London Suburb*, unpublished M.Phil thesis, University of Leeds, 1973.

Brook, G. L., 'The Future of English Dialect Studies', *Studies in honour of Harold Orton*, Leeds Studies in English, Vol. II, 1968.

Chomsky, N., *Current Issues in Linguistic Theory*, Janua Linguarum No. 38, Mouton & Co., The Hague, 1964.

Chomsky, N. and Halle, M., *The Sound Pattern of English*, Harper & Row, New York, 1968.

Fudge, E. C., 'The Nature of Phonological Primes', *Journal of Linguistics*, Vol. 3, 1967.

Fudge, E. C. (ed.), *Phonology*, Penguin Books, 1973.

Gibson, P. H., *Studies in the Linguistic Geography of Staffordshire*, unpublished M.A. thesis, University of Leeds, 1955.

Gilliéron, J. and Edmont, E., *Atlas linguistique de la France*, Paris, 1902–10.

Gimson, A. C., *An Introduction to the Pronunciation of English* (2nd edition), Edward Arnold Ltd., London, 1970.

Heath, C. D., *A Study of Speech Patterns in the Urban District of Cannock, Staffordshire*, unpublished Ph.D. thesis, University of Leeds, 1971.

H.M.S.O., *Classification of Occupations 1966*, General Register Office.

Houck, C. L., 'Methodology of an Urban Speech Survey', *Studies in honour of Harold Orton*, Leeds Studies in English, Vol. II, 1968.

International Phonetic Association, *The Principles of the International Phonetic Association*, London, 1949, reprinted 1964.

Jones, D., *An Outline of English Phonetics* (8th edition), W. Heffer & Sons Ltd., Cambridge, 1956.

Jones, D., *The Phoneme: its Nature and Use* (2nd edition), W. Heffer & Sons Ltd., Cambridge, 1962.

Joos, M., *Acoustic Phonetics*, Language Monograph No. 23, Linguistic Society of America, Baltimore, 1948.

Knowles, G., *A Discussion of Houck's Dialectology*, unpublished paper, 1968.

Kökeritz, H., *The Phonology of the Suffolk Dialect*, Uppsala, 1932.

Martinet, A., 'De la morphonologie', *La Linguistique*, No. 1, 1965. Extracts reprinted under title: 'Morphophonemics' in *Phonology* (see above); translated by the editor.

Orton, H., *Survey of English Dialects: Introduction*, University of Leeds, 1962 (includes the Dieth-Orton questionnaire).

Orton, H. et al., *Survey of English Dialects: Basic Material*, University of Leeds, 1962–71.

Pike, K. L., *Phonemics*, University of Michigan Press, 1947.

Prins, A. A., *A History of English Phonemes*, Leiden University Press, 1972.

Roberts, J. E., *Bilberry Pie*, Cannock Chase Literary Society, 1964.

Roberts, J. E., *More Bilberry Pie*, Cannock Chase Literary Society, 1966.

Sapir, E., 'Sound patterns in language', *Language*, Vol. 1, 1925. Reprinted in *Phonology* (see above).

Schane, S. A., *French Phonology and Morphology*, Research Monograph No. 45, Massachusetts Institute of Technology, 1968.

Sivertsen, E., *Cockney Phonology*, Oslo University Press, 1960.

Wakelin, M., *English Dialects: an Introduction*, Athlone Press, 1972.

Wells, J. C., 'Local Accents in England and Wales', *Journal of Linguistics*, Vol. 6, 1970.

Index

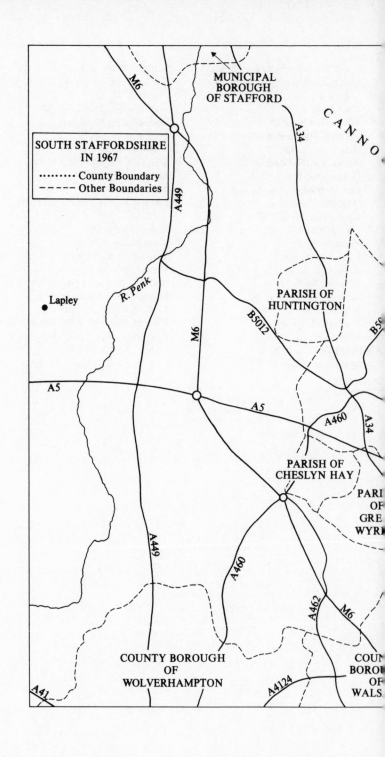

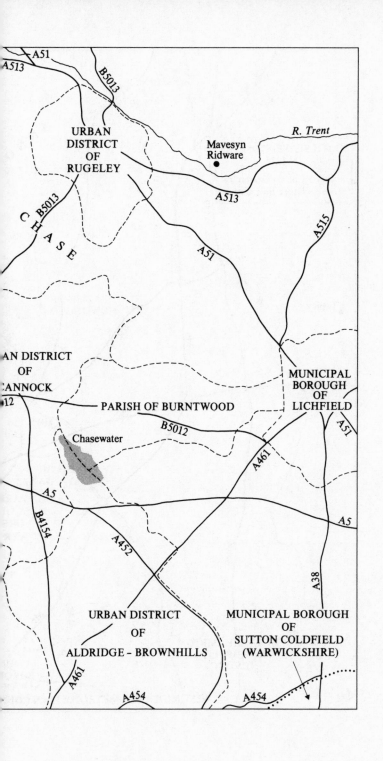

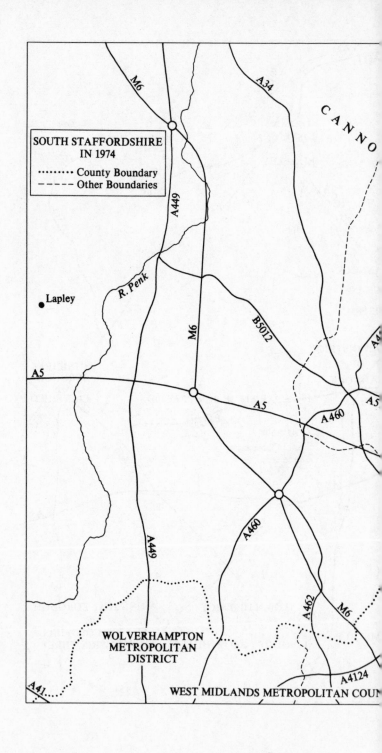

SOUTH STAFFORDSHIRE
IN 1974
·········· County Boundary
------ Other Boundaries

M6

A34

CANNO

A449

R. Penk

•Lapley

M6

BS012

A5

A5

A460

A5

A449

A460

A462

M6

WOLVERHAMPTON
METROPOLITAN
DISTRICT

A41

A4124

WEST MIDLANDS METROPOLITAN COUN

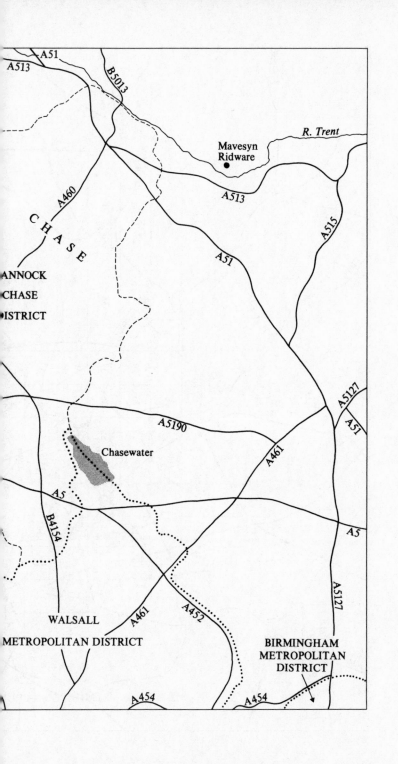

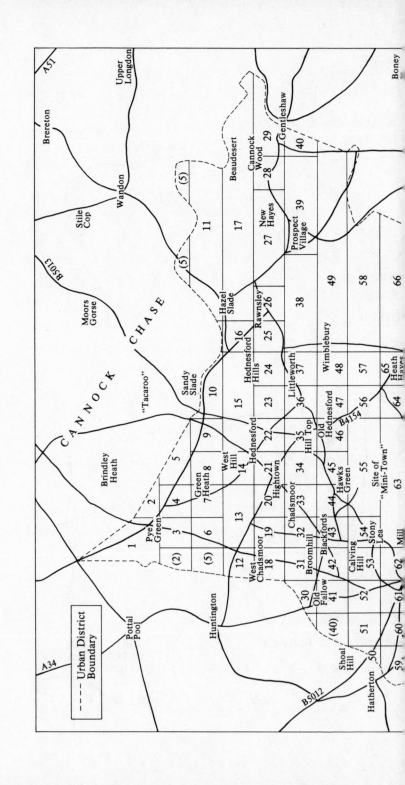

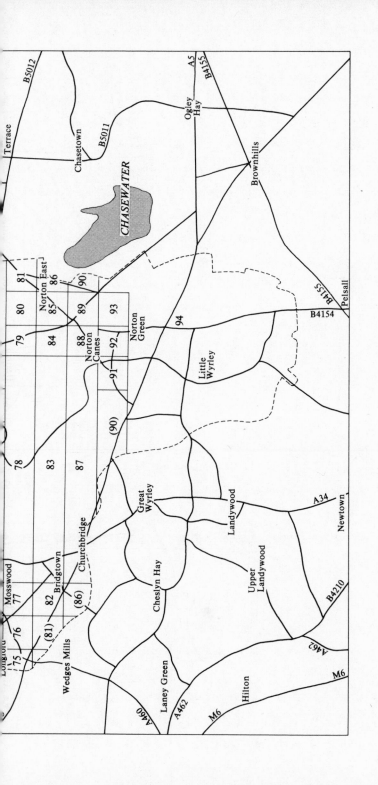